D0926124

Drawings by Baker Lake Artists

Where the River Widens

Qamanittuaq

Marion Jackson, Judith Nasby and William Noah

Macdonald Stewart Art Centre, Guelph, Ontario

ᑎᑎᕐᖅᐅᔅᕐᑕᐅᓂᖑᑦ

ᖅᑲᓗᓂᑐᐊᖅᖅ

ᖅᑲᓗᓂᑐᐊᖅᖳᒥ ᑎᑎᕐᖅᐅᔅᖳᑎᓄᑦ

Luke Anguhadluq
Irene Avaalaaqiaq
Marjorie Esa
Martha Ittuluka'naaq
Hannah Kigusiuq
Janet Kigusiuq
Myra Kukiiyaut
Victoria Mamnguqsualuk
William Noah
Françoise Oklaga
Jessie Oonark
Nancy Pukingrnak
Harold Qarliqsaq
Ruth Qaulluaryuk
Armand Tagoona
Simon Tookoome
Ruth Annaqtuusi Tulurialik
Marion Tuu'luuq
Mark Uqayuittuq

ᑐᑭᓯ ᐊᐧᔪᓛᑐᖅ
ᐊᐃᕆᓐ ᐊᕙᓚᖅᐊᖅ
ᒪᕐᔨ ᐃᓴ
ᒪᕐᑕ ᐃᑦᑐᓛᑲᖅ
ᕼᐊᓇ ᑭᒍᓯᐅᖅ
ᔮᓇᑦ ᑭᒍᓯᐅᖅ
ᒪᐃᕋ ᑯᑭᔭᐅᑦ
ᐃᑦᑐᕆᐧ ᒪᒻᒍᖅᐊᓗᒃ
ᕆᐊᓪ ᓄᐊ
ᐊᖅᓯ ᐅᖅᑲᒐᖅ
ᔨᓯ ᐅᐱᖅᓇᖅ
ᓇᓯ ᐳᑭᖅᓇ ᖅ
ᕼᐱ ᖃᑦᖅᒃᖅ
ᕈᑎ ᖃᐅᓗᐊᖅᓕᒃ
ᐊᖅᒪᓐ ᑕᑰᖅᓇᑦᔅ
ᓴᐃᒪᓐ ᑐᑯᒥ
ᕈᑎ ᐊᓇᖅᑐᓯ ᑐᓗᕆᐊᓕᒃ
ᒦᐅᕆᔅ ᑐᑦᓗᖅ
ᒪᖅᑭ ᐅᖅᑲᐧᑐᖅ

An exhibition
organized and circu-
lated by the Macdonald
Stewart Art Centre with support
from Blount Canada Ltd.; the Museums
Assistance Program of Canadian Heritage; the
Ministry of Economic Development and Tourism of
the Government of the Northwest Territories through
Qatqamiut: The Baker Lake Historical Society; the Ontario Arts
Council; the Jackman Foundation; Calm Air International Ltd.
and Canadian North and private donations.

INUIT ART FROM THE MACDONALD STEWART ART CENTRE COLLECTION

Since 1980 the Macdonald Stewart Art Centre has acquired over 400 drawings by Canadian Inuit artists. These works date from the early 1960s to the present and are complemented with examples of other major Inuit art media. Generous sponsorship from Blount Canada Ltd., which donated purchase funds in 1980, enabled the Art Centre to begin this specialized collection. Blount Canada Ltd. of Guelph (formerly Omark Canada Ltd.) is a manufacturer in the timber harvesting industry and is owned by Blount Inc., whose international headquarters are in Montgomery, Alabama. The Art Centre has benefited from the continuing support of this company and its General Manager, Nicholas Galovich and former General Manager, K.O. Hammill who retired in 1994. Blount Canada Ltd.'s contribution to the Art Centre was recognized in 1987 by the Ontario Association of Art Galleries' Corporate Award of Merit.

Additional art purchase funds for Inuit art have been provided by The Canada Council, the Ontario Government through the Ministry of Culture, Tourism and Recreation and by the Art Centre Volunteers. The Centre has also been fortunate to receive gifts of art from numerous individuals and groups in Canada and abroad.

The Art Centre's research and collecting activities have benefited from grants received from the Museum Assistance Program of Canadian Heritage which supported Judith Nasby's research and acquisition trips to the Eastern and Central Arctic, and Marion Jackson's research in Baker Lake. Support was also received from The Canada Council through the Visual Arts Section Programme Grant for Public Galleries which sponsored research trips by Jackson and Nasby in 1993 and Art Centre staff in 1994.

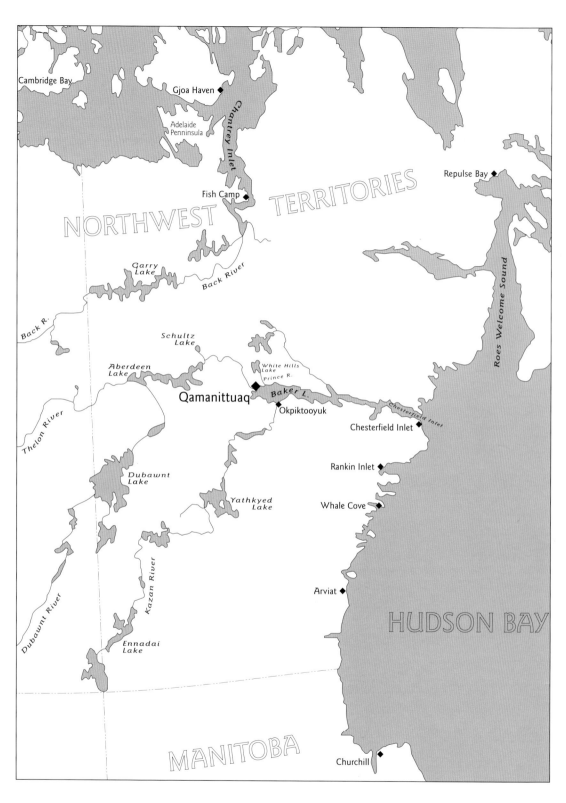

Map of Keewatin District, Northwest Territories - Qamanittuaq (Baker Lake), centrally located in the Keewatin District, is also the geographic centre of Canada.

PREFACE AND ACKNOWLEDGMENTS

The Macdonald Stewart Art Centre is recognized internationally for its collection of contemporary Inuit drawings and for its leadership in exhibiting and promoting scholarship on these works. Among world institutions collecting Inuit art, the Art Centre is unique in its focus on building a specialized collection of drawings. The collection began in 1980 with support from the Guelph company Blount Canada Ltd. Today, the collection contains about 400 drawings as well as sculpture, prints, printstones, wall-hangings and clothing.

The Art Centre's touring exhibition, *Contemporary Inuit Drawings* (1987) was the first survey exhibition of drawings from settlements across the Canadian Arctic. It brought new and serious attention to drawing as a major artistic medium of the Canadian Inuit. Inuit sculpture and prints had been similarly showcased in previous international exhibitions: *Sculpture/Inuit: Masterworks of the Canadian Arctic* (Canadian Eskimo Arts Council, 1971) and *The Inuit Print/L'estampe Inuit* (National Museum of Man, National Museums of Canada, 1977).

To build on previous work and as a further refinement of research, the Art Centre has organized this exhibition of drawings from the community of Baker Lake. The exhibition presents visually compelling works by major Baker Lake artists illustrating the highly individualistic approaches of these artists and the unusually rich heritage of shamanistic and traditional spirit imagery from which they draw their inspiration. Drawings have been selected from the Macdonald Stewart Art Centre's collection of Baker Lake drawings which is documented with invaluable commentary by the artists.

The title for the exhibition *Where the River Widens* has a double meaning, referring both to the English translation of *Qamanittuaq* (the Inuit name for Baker Lake) and connecting the confluence of cultural influences (Inuit and southern) that created the context in which the drawings were produced during the past 35 years. *Where the River Widens* will enhance viewers' appreciation for the unique and highly expressive art of Baker Lake and will help them to understand how Baker Lake drawings relate to but differ from drawings from other Inuit communities. The exhibition has been organized with the substantial involvement of the artists.

I would like to thank the artists for their enthusiasm and good will toward all aspects of the research and presentation of the exhibition. It was a pleasure as well for me to work with my co-curators for the exhibition, Marion Jackson and William Noah, on the selection of drawings and writing of the catalogue which is the result of a research and acquisition phase stretching over more than a decade. We also appreciate the participation of Peter Millard, Professor Emeritus of the University of Saskatchewan, for contributing an interpretive essay to the catalogue.

A number of organizations and individuals provided assistance: I would particularly like to mention the members of *Qatqamiut:* The Baker Lake Historical Society who staged the very successful Baker Lake Art Symposium in August 1994. It was a significant and rewarding experience for Art Centre staff members, Nancy Campbell (Curator), Stephen Robinson (Programs Co-ordinator) and Verne Harrison (Preparator), to participate in the symposium held in Baker Lake.

Many individuals assisted with the project. It would be difficult to name all of them but I would like to acknowledge Marie Bouchard, Nellie Peryouar and David Tagoona, Mayor of Baker Lake. Terry Vanderschaaf and his staff at the Jessie Oonark Arts and Crafts Centre in Baker Lake produced a T-shirt to commemorate the exhibition tour. Ingo Hessel and Jeanne L'Espérance, of the Inuit Art Section of Indian and Northern Affairs Canada, provided information from which Sheila Ord, independent studies student (University of Guelph Fine Art Department), compiled the artists' biographies for the catalogue. Julie Gibb and Christian Morrison of GreenStreet Design were responsible for the distinctive design of the catalogue. Calm Air International Ltd. and Canadian North donated airfare for William Noah to attend the exhibition opening in Guelph. I would also like to thank Samuel and Esther Sarick for their support.

Art Centre staff members were a significant part of the production team. Verne Harrison co-ordinated the display and art traffic arrangements and photography provided by Julianna Murphy, Martin Schwalbe and the University of Guelph's Office for Educational Practice. The exhibition and art symposium also provided lasting educational material which will be useful for orientation programs co-ordinated by Stephen Robinson. Documentary video footage taken by Verne Harrison added significant reference material to our archives about the symposium and artist interviews. Joanne Bullock was responsible for data entry and word processing and Gregory Klages was responsible for promotion. Administrative and secretarial requirements were contributed by Sorouja Williamson and Tiffany Gemnich respectively. I would like to thank all of the Art Centre staff members for their valuable contributions to the realization of the project.

The Macdonald Stewart Art Centre was fortunate to receive generous funding for the exhibition tour from the Museums Assistance Program of Canadian Heritage and from the Ministry of Economic Development and Tourism of the Government of the Northwest Territories through *Qatqamiut:* The Baker Lake Historical Society. We are grateful as well to the Ontario Arts Council and to the Jackman Foundation for sponsoring the publication. We are principally indebted to the artists, whose vision and dedication have produced these remarkable drawings which will be enjoyed by gallery visitors across Canada.

Judith Nasby
Director

CELEBRATING THE OPENING
OF THE EXHIBITION AT THE
BAKER LAKE ART SYMPOSIUM

JUDITH NASBY

A caribou sinew rope was cut with ulus, traditional women's knives, to open this exhibition of drawings in the community hall of Baker Lake, Northwest Territories on August 19, 1994. The exhibition featured 43 drawings by 19 artists representing 35 years of drawing activity in Baker Lake. This is the first survey exhibition of Baker Lake drawings to be organized and the first touring exhibition produced by a Southern gallery to open in an Arctic settlement. The complete exhibition containing 77 works from the Macdonald Stewart Art Centre Collection will comprise the touring version to be shown at galleries across Canada over the next two years.

The Baker Lake showing of *Qamanittuaq: Where the River Widens* was of particular significance to the twelve living artists represented in the exhibition, all of whom attended the opening. The twelve artists: Irene Avaalaaqiaq, Marjorie Esa, Hannah Kigusiuq, Janet Kigusiuq, Myra Kukiiyaut, Victoria Mamnguqsualuk, William Noah, Nancy Pukingrnak, Ruth Qaulluaryuk, Simon Tookoome, Ruth Annaqtuusi Tulurialik and Marion Tuu'luuq participated in the opening festivities. Highlights were drum dancing, throat singing, a demonstration of dog team whip skills by artist Simon Tookoome, and singing in Inuktitut by artist Ruth Annaqtuusi Tulurialik and her husband Hugh Tulurialik, who accompanied on guitar. For the artists, this occasion was the first opportunity to see their own and fellow artists' work in an exhibition context. Many had never seen their drawings matted and framed. Unlike the situation in the South where artists have ample opportunity to see each other's work, the tradition in the Arctic has been for the art to go directly from the artist's hand to Southern markets via the Arctic co-operatives or through dealers. There has been so little opportunity for artists and the community to see the art works that many children in a settlement like Baker Lake are unaware that their grandparents are famous artists respected internationally.

The artists spoke about their art and concerns about being practising artists during the concurrent art symposium which was organized by *Qatqamiut: The Baker Lake Historical Society*. Artist William Noah emphasized the significance of the drawing collection's coming to Baker Lake saying, "the exhibition provides a history of 35 years of art making in Baker Lake and is a great stimulus for the artists to continue producing." He drew attention to the unfortunate closure of the Baker Lake printshop in 1990 and the inability of the community to produce annual collections of stonecut and stencil prints since that time. He commented, "It is a tragedy that our world famous print collections ceased production from a combination of funding and administrative problems. Those with experience need to come together to create a new collection of prints." He emphasised the need for an influx of money for start-up costs since the former printshop has been dismantled and turned into a grocery store. With the closure of the printshop there has been

an unfortunate corresponding reduction in the number of drawings being produced in Baker Lake, since original drawings are the sources for the stonecut and stencil prints.

The art symposium was attended by 30 participants including curators from leading Southern public galleries holding Inuit art as well as writers and collectors from Canada and the United States. In a forum for artists and curators a number of artists commented that Inuit artists often don't understand the intricacies of the Southern marketing system that promotes and distributes their work. William Noah noted that many Inuit works have been sold in the past without recording the artist's description of the subject and that this must change. He added ironically, "It is often the piece the artist likes the least that the Southern buyer selects, being attracted to a roughly finished sculpture. The piece the artist has carefully finished and attached a story to is turned down. This can be discouraging to the artist." Artist Hannah Kigusiuq said it was critical that the Northern dealers and cooperatives stay active since most artists, especially the older ones, do not speak English and are unfamiliar with Southern business practices.

The symposium program was planned to focus on the artists, the community and the tundra landscape. In addition to the exhibition of drawings, there was a showing of 40 recent wall hangings held in the high school gymnasium. Appliqué and embroidered wall hangings are a distinctive and highly developed Baker Lake medium involving a number of prolific women artists including Irene Avaalaaqiaq, Ruth Qualluaryuk, Janet Kigusiuq and Victoria Mamnguqsualuk who are represented in this drawing exhibition. At a traditional banquet, some of the artists and other residents provided direct evidence of their high level of sewing skills by exhibiting a variety of garments ranging from the magnificent beaded caribou *amautiq* (parka) to more contemporary versions incorporating aspects of the *amautiq* design with Southern styles.

Symposium participants and residents attended a session to hear the twelve artists interviewed in turn about the subject matter of their drawings in the Macdonald Stewart Art Centre exhibition. Sessions were also held on the history of the community and the Inuktitut language. Many participants attended community events including a wedding feast, traditional square dancing, church services in Inuktitut and a traditional camp where an Inuit family explained and demonstrated summer camp domestic skills. Elementary and secondary school students attended exhibition tours and participated in the opening ceremonies by serving refreshments.

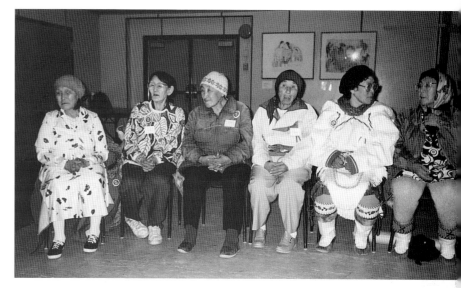

Direct benefits to the community were the dialogue between participants, artists and the community at large, research and artist interviews and art sales to public and private collections. A Canada Council Art Bank jury, held concurrently with the symposium, purchased sculpture, drawings and seven major wall hangings for this national collection which rents art to government and publicly operated institutions. A number of young Inuit who served on the symposium organizing committee or who chaired sessions gained valuable administrative experience from the event, the first of its kind in this settlement of 1,200 people.

The exhibition *Qamanittuaq: Where the River Widens* is presented in the context of previous publications on Inuit drawings by the Art Centre. Our intention has been to build a specialized collection that would represent drawing by major Inuit artists in those communities where art making has included a drawing program. The collection contains approximately 400 drawings dating from 1960 onward. Many public collections of Inuit art have grown primarily through donations; whereas the Art Centre's collection has been built through carefully focused purchases. The majority of the drawings in this exhibition were acquired in the early 1980s and others were selected from the Sanavik Co-operative archives in Baker Lake or directly from the artists during a research trip in 1993.

It was important to hold the opening of the exhibition tour in Baker Lake to further our association with the artists and to highlight the fundamental involvement William Noah has had as one of the co-curators for this exhibition. Forty-three of the drawings, as indicated by an ulu symbol (⟁) in the catalogue entries, were displayed in Baker Lake during the five-day art symposium. The majority of the 1,200 residents visited the community hall to see the drawings which were hung chronologically by artist according to the date of birth. As a result the twelve artists who attended and the relatives and descendants of the deceased artists gained a clear impression of the history of drawing in Baker Lake and of those individuals who were prominent in its development.

The chronological hanging order also continues an organization method introduced in the touring exhibition *Contemporary Inuit Drawings*, organized by the Macdonald Stewart Art Centre in 1987. This chronological or "generational approach" for organizing the drawings was devised by Carleton University art historian, Marion Jackson. Jackson was co-curator with Judith Nasby for the *Contemporary Inuit Drawings* exhibition which presented a survey of prominent artists from across the Arctic and brought to public attention the importance of drawing as a major Inuit art medium.

As an interpretive method, the generational model helps to provide insight into Inuit drawings which are so different from the Western tradition of draftsmanship based on naturalistic perspective. The older artists, most of whom are now deceased, began drawing in the 1960s after living most of their lives on the land hunting and fishing for their food. Their thought patterns were conditioned by this nomadic life style and the traditional religion which emphasized the duality of physical and spiritual realities in human, animal and natural forces. Jackson pointed out shared characteristics in the drawings of these "first generation artists": the use of repetition (much like hunting tallies); the isolation of images on a page without specific context; a blending of perspectives and a predominance of "transformation" subjects.

Jackson noted certain other characteristics common to the next generation of artists, who came into settlements and into sustained contact with white society earlier in their lives. Among these younger artists, there is a tendency, on the one hand, to provide more specific information regarding the experience of the Inuit culture and its traditional myths or, on the other hand, to move toward a more conscious expression of aesthetic qualities. Jackson attributed this difference between generations to an increasing consciousness of "self as artist" among the younger Inuit artists. This generational approach had meaning as well for William Noah from the standpoint of his own involvement in art making in Baker Lake and his place in its history. In both his drawings (No. 74-77) and his autobiographical essay, he consciously and carefully records his experiences and expresses the values and sensibilities of his culture.

Our relationship with William Noah has been an important component of continuing research on the 200 Baker Lake drawings we are fortunate to have in the collection. Noah worked closely with Marion Jackson when she was conducting extensive research in Baker Lake in 1983 and 1985, acting as translator of artist interviews. Being a relative and a close associate of many of the artists, Noah could best provide the nuances of translation required to capture the intent of the artists.

The rationale for the selection of works was to choose representative drawings by prominent artists working in this medium. The exhibition is therefore representative, rather than definitive. It presents examples of work by 19 artists organized in a manner to convey an impression of the history of drawing in Baker Lake over the past 35 years.

A significant contribution to the publication are the catalogue notes written by Marion Jackson based on the 1983 manuscript she and William Noah produced from their interviews with 19 artists who talked to them about specific drawings in the Art Centre collection. Jackson was one of the few art historians to interview Jessie Oonark before she died in 1985. Subsequent interviews conducted with artists in 1993 and at the Baker Lake Art Symposium have been cited in the catalogue notes.

Both Jackson and Noah have contributed essays reflecting on the history and the development of the art programs in Baker Lake. Their essays provide two very different views of this history. Noah's essay is autobiographical and gives an engaging, poetic and personal insight into the lived experience of an artist in the community. Jackson's essay, on the other hand, is a scholarly documentation of events from the point of view of a researcher looking at the community from outside. The two essays are complementary and not only combine to give a view of the history of Baker Lake, but also stand as testimony to the fruitfulness of collaboration across cultural boundaries. An essay by Peter Millard, Professor Emeritus of English at the University of Saskatchewan, draws on the considerable insight Professor Millard has gained from studying and collecting Inuit art for more than three decades. He discusses some of the distinctive characteristics of Inuit drawings which are different from the Western drawing tradition and some of the attitudes Southern viewers bring to their consideration of Inuit Art.

The catalogue will be a lasting commentary on this 35 year period in the history of drawing in Baker Lake. The art symposium was an enormous impetus to the artists and to those in the community who help administer and market their art internationally. The exhibition has given the artists their first opportunity to see their own work in the context of their community's art history. How will this experience affect their world view and motivation to contribute as individual artists to the continuation of this rich history? Certainly in the past the annual print collections have been a major motivation for the production of drawings. It is hoped that the success of the exhibition and art symposium in Baker Lake will stimulate the resumption of the annual print collections, which together with wall hangings and sculpture have brought international acclaim to the artists of Baker Lake.

STARVATION ON THE LAND AND MY EXPERIENCE IN BAKER LAKE

WILLIAM NOAH

Starvation on the Land After my father died, we had no one to look after us, and I was too young to look after myself. There were my mother, Mary, Peggy, Nancy and myself. We had relatives, but they had their own families to look after as well as looking after us. After going back and forth among each of our relatives, it got worse and worse and finally unbearable.

Our men had gone to Baker Lake and had just come back with bad news that one of Luke Anguhadluq's sons had been shot with a rifle while the young people were playing outside the iglus. Anguhadluq's family was living near White Hills Lake, not too far from Baker Lake. My brother was married to the sister of the young man who was shot. My brother and his family were in great sadness and said they were going to move to Anguhadluq's camp. My mother asked me if I would like to go with them when they were moving down. I agreed to go even though I was then thirteen years of age and had never been separated from my mother before. It was really scary for me to go and leave my mother.

Our very first travelling day was okay, but the next day we travelled all day and when we were about to camp – just maybe an hour and a half before we would stop – the snow started to drift a little and it got really chilly. It can chill to the bones when it is really cold even though we were wearing caribou clothing. We were cold and hungry at the same time. My sister-in-law was leading and running in front of the dogs, some way ahead of us. For some reason, I got off the sled and was running, but the dogs were too fast for me and I got way behind for a while, maybe too far behind. My brother and his wife finally stopped and waited for me to catch up, and when I caught up we camped and settled down for the night.

After a few days of travel, we reached Luke Anguhadluq's camp which is not too far from White Hills Lake. I remember so well that day. When we reached that camp, it was a very beautiful day – calm and the sky was so clear – but the sadness was yet to come. We reached Luke Anguhadluq's camp just as the sun was setting. We stopped in front of their iglu, and we all went inside. The grown people started weeping and crying over the young man who was to be my brother-in-law. The young man who had been shot had been promised to my sister Nancy to be her husband when they got old enough, but now he was dead, never to be seen again and not to be brought back to life. After great sorrow and weeping and crying our eyes out, I moved into the house or iglu of my other sister, Mary Yusipik, who was married to Norman Segaqtii, to stay as long as I was welcome.

There was still a great confusion and sadness very much in my heart because I had left my mother and sister Nancy back at Back River. And there was no food at all at the time I left them behind. Most of the time, they were all by themselves with no food, and there was no guarantee that they would be looked after properly by my uncle Samson Quinanaaq because he was always so busy out hunting and fishing with his wife Elizabeth.

Even though I was now happily living with my brother-in-law Norman with plenty of food most of the time – although still with lack of food from time to time – I was not comfortable. So when some people from that camp started to go to Baker Lake to get some supplies and to tell the RCMP to go and pick up my mother and sister by the RCMP plane, I went along to make sure that the RCMP would go and look for them. There were other camps that had died from starvation in the Garry Lake area, and the famine was greatly spreading all across the North. We had heard that we were not the only people who were about to starve.

We spent a day-and-a-half or so in Baker Lake. Then my brother-in-law, Norman, and I started back for Norman's camp at Oqsuliinaaq. I don't remember whether my brother came along with us or stayed with the RCMP to go look for my mother and sister Nancy, I am not sure. In a few days the RCMP went to look for my mother and sister and found them alive but just barely alive and very hungry and cold.

And then I heard the good news that my mother and sister were then in Baker Lake and that my brother and the special constable had made a nice little snow house for them down at the shoreline right in front of the RCMP house and office. In a few days, I was very anxious to go to Baker Lake to be with my own mother and sister once more, so Norman took me down to Baker Lake to be with them. When we reached Baker Lake, I started to look for my mother's snow house. It was dark along the shoreline of Baker Lake, and I had never been alone before so I was a little bit scared. I found the snow house with a white dog inside, and I recognized my own white dog and was really surprised to see it still alive and staying inside the iglu.

Baker Lake in the 1950s and 1960s

Before that time, I used to come to Baker Lake sometimes to get supplies or just to visit to watch people unloading the ship, but just a few times. I never wanted to stay in Baker Lake then. I moved to Baker Lake only because I had no choice but to go to school and avoid the starvation in 1957 and 1958.

When I first moved into Baker Lake, there were only a few houses. There was an Anglican mission house. It was much smaller than today. Even the church was much shorter. Both of them are still standing. There was a Hudson's Bay store, a staff house, and one or two warehouses to go with them. There was a Roman Catholic house and their church next to it. Far off was the RCMP house with the staff house and the old steel frame warehouse. I don't think the nursing station was even built in those years.

Way down eastward were the MOT (Ministry of Transport) and the DOT (Department of Transport) staff houses, maybe four or five houses. They were, it seemed, the richest people with one or two Inuit employees. The Inuit employees seemed to make a lot of money, up to $1.00 per day or $2.00 per day and it went up higher in no time too. There was one big house being used by Mitkeayuuq who was working for the weather station and his family. It was located where the public four-bedroom housing is today.

Later on William Aupaluktuq built his own one-room house after he got married to my sister Nancy. Louis Tapatai was living in a house too. He seemed to have lots of money and lots of things belonging to him. He was working for DOT or MOT. The MOT and DOT had one big long building with a pool table and some rooms where they operated the high frequency radios, some bunk beds and all, and two or three Inuit ladies working for them – kitchen helpers, cook, and janitor. That was the biggest employer in Baker

Lake. Louis Tapatai was a caterpillar operator for MOT. Armand Tagoona and his family were living in the large house which was later occupied by Mitkeayuuq after Armand Tagoona left for Rankin Inlet to become an Anglican minister.

Lastly there was the public day school where I was to be the day after I arrived in Baker Lake. It was one large room, 40 by 80 feet or even more. Later on, the teachers' and the area administrators' houses were built. That was the beginning of Baker Lake. There were people also who were working for the Hudson's Bay Company.

Titus Naigo had his small house too and Thomas Tapatai, who was a catechist for the Anglican mission, had a fine-looking small house. He welcomed strangers who were coming to the town who may have been half-starving or may have travelled all day by dog team in the very cold weather. All Inuit newcomers knew where to go for food and drink. As soon as they arrived, he helped a lot of people. This was Baker Lake in the 1950s and early 1960s.

My Move to Baker Lake I didn't want to live in Baker Lake at first, but I settled down and it became my hometown when I was 13 years of age. I did not like it at first because the young men and even the grown men would gang up on me. Secondly, there was no place to go to eat country food, nobody to hunt and fish for us. Almost every day we were half-starving, but when we learned to work we were able to survive. We went to school with empty stomachs, went to church with no food in our stomachs because no one was permitted to stay home unless they were really sick.

Every single one of the people went to church when it was time to go. The Minister, Reverend Canon James, would go after you if you missed one service, and you'd better have some good explanations for him if you missed one church service. The Bay manager was also strict. And the Anglican minister was strict. I don't know too much about the R.C. Mission priests. They were very kind, that's all. The teachers were very strict too. We had to run to school, not be a minute late. No chewing gum in school. Speak English only. Even if we couldn't speak English, we had to try hard!

Most Baker Lake people in those days used to gang up on the newcomers or outsiders. Even the adults were really mean and made a lot of fun of us newcomers. I know one or two people who used to slap my back as hard as they could, and it used to really hurt. In those days, like any other time, some of the people were really bad, not every one of them though. That is one reason why I did not wish to move to Baker Lake before, but now it is my hometown, and I'm happy to live here and am loving it all.

Artwork In the late 1950s carvings were considered by the Inuit to be no more than toys for the children, and our parents used to make them just for their children. They made them for free for their children. They were not for sale to anyone because they were not made for grown-ups. If some would ask for a toy from the adults – especially an adult asking another adult for a toy – it would have been really silly. Well, that is exactly what happened to my mother when Andy Macpherson, the wildlife biologist, asked my mother to make a drawing on a piece of paper, to make a drawing for him to take with him. After that, she continued to keep on making drawings and to hand the drawings over to Mr. Dodds who was a DIAND (Department of Indian Affairs and Northern Development) officer here in Baker Lake. To us – to my mother and me – we wondered why the white people would want a piece of paper with some funny drawings on them. We thought those papers were useless. Later, we were informed that in the community of Cape Dorset, they were making drawings and about to start making prints out of the drawings, and my mother's works were to be included with Cape Dorset's works.

My mother was a very perceptive person, and whenever she would see a person who was needing new clothing, she would make them without asking for payment in return. Maybe that is how she got noticed for her wonderful works and artistic skills. After that time, she did countless drawings and wall hangings.

After a while when some craft officers and art advisers started to come up north and ask grownup Inuit to make antler carvings and to try to make some drawings, it was surprising to us. Like I said earlier, that was just part of a toy-making thing for the Inuit. But the *Qabloonaq* did not seem to care if it was silly or not to make antler carvings. Some of us tried to make some drawings and some of us tried to make caribou antler carvings even though it was hard for us. Not everyone is a carver or an artist.

In the early 1960s, people needed money to go to the moving pictures, so they learned to make rough carvings in no time at all. They did not really care if they got famous or not; they just wanted a dollar to go to the movies, or a dime and a nickel to buy a chocolate bar, a dime to buy a can of pop, 50 cents to buy cigarettes. In those days, we survived with $250 a month. The DOT and MOT were making $1,000 a month. They were the richest in the world!

When the 1970s arrived, we were able to make drawings, and some were able to make carvings too. That's the time the Government's Craft Shop was opened, and Sheila and Jack Butler became the greatest art advisors of all times. They started teaching people how to make prints. Before the Butlers came, people in Baker Lake were asked to try to make prints but they were

never serious about it. In the early 1970s, people started taking printmaking more seriously. That's the time Baker Lake artists hit the top for a while, but not for long because the Government Craft Shop lasted only three or four years. In 1977 the Government Craft Shop burned to the ground, and the artists and printers lost millions of dollars worth of artworks and prints and carvings. After that time, the new Co-op building was built and people started making new prints all over again, but things were never the same. Later the Co-op became a grocery store, and buying of art work and making prints was dropped and forgotten.

My Works as an Artist When we were young we used to make images on the ice windows, but our parents used to tell us not to make marks on the snow walls or the ice window, so we had to listen to them. One day though I was asked to make some drawings. In 1970 or 1971, I was approached by some people asking if I would be interested in becoming a printmaker, so I tried and I thought it was worthwhile to keep working as a printmaker. I kept on trying and I got heavily involved in the co-op movement for seven or eight years. After that, I got into politics, travelled heavily, and almost destroyed myself in a way.

In artwork, I have tried all kinds of different ways of making prints, drawings, paintings – a few on canvas, on plywood, silk-screening, and others things too. Most of the arts and the images that I made are from my own past experience in my life. I love to make animal drawings because that is what we lived on in the old days. Landscapes that I do are because I see the land every single day. There are no trees, so I can see miles and miles around, once I get on top of a hill or mountain.

Later I didn't have time to make drawings for any individual or any art galleries. I have four sons, two daughters, six dogs, and I am busy looking after the independent Christian Church. For a while, I did freelancing for CBC Rankin Inlet radio which broadcasts throughout the North. In the 1980s, I worked as the Regional Program Manager for the Inuit Broadcasting Corporation which we call IBC for short, and I built my own three-bedroom house which I started in August 1988. Also, I am busy looking after the fish nets.

Technology: The Computer Equipment In the middle of 1994, computers were introduced to the Inuit of Baker Lake who were trained to use Corel Draw 4.0. The last training took place August 2-19, 1994, on the Corel 5.0. The first Corel Draw 4.0 was quite fascinating to a beginner on computerized equipment which the Inuit have never had the opportunity to experience or even to dream about before. It did not especially go with my personality. One time I got so frustrated that I punched the table in my frustrations, and you can guess my next target. Luckily he was much heavier than I! I am not encouraging the same experience for others.

Even though things did not work out for me at the training session, I was ahead of myself when I got to the Paintshop software. I got into the artwork right away and did some painting of the landscape with a tent and a beautiful river running by.

I would like to convince people who have no hopes – especially the native people – that some of us will be doing artwork with the computers before we know it. I have done three beautiful paintings on the Paintshop in both Corel Draw 4.0 and Corel Draw 5.0. The three paintings are *The Campsite, The Autumn Leaves* and *The Ptarmigan*. The *Ptarmigan* that I painted with the Corel Draw 4.0 was made into a limited edition of 10 silkscreen prints. It is the first time ever to make a print from a painting from Corel Draw 4.0 and the first painting ever done by an Inuk graphic designer right here in Baker Lake.

We have been told hundreds of times before not to use electronic equipment, but I have found out now that, no matter what I use, my style does not change. Whether I use my hands or the computer, my style is still there. My style does not change.

This essay combines a text written by William Noah expressly for this exhibition catalogue, an excerpt from his forthcoming autobiography and excerpts from a speech he delivered at the opening of the Baker Lake Art Symposium in August 1994.

Map showing the three main Inuit groups relocated to Qamanittuaq (Baker Lake) in the 1950s and 1960s

The **Netsilik Inuit** included the *Uqusiksilingmiut, Ualingmiut, Lluliagmiut* and *Saningayukmiut;* the **Caribou Inuit** included the *Qainigmiut, Akilniaqmiut, Havauqtormiut, Padleimiut* and coastal dwelling *Tariaqmiut;* and the **Iglulik Inuit** were represented by a few Aivilingmiut settlers.

QAMANITTUAQ:
WHERE THE RIVER WIDENS

MARION JACKSON

The vast tundra lying west of Hudson Bay, today known as the Keewatin District, is characterized by rolling plateaus with intermittent slow-rising hills and sand eskers, interlaced by a rich system of rivers and inland lakes. The excessively strong winds ("Keewatin" being the Cree word for "the North Wind") and extreme winters give this area one of the harshest climates on the North American continent. Nevertheless, the area has been a site of intermittent and increasing cultural interchange during the past four centuries. British navigators explored the coast of the Keewatin District in their search for the Northwest Passage in the 17th century, with Sir Thomas Button reaching the mouth of the Chesterfield Inlet in 1612/13 and Captain Luke Foxe mapping the west coast of Hudson Bay in the 1630s. Following the formation of the Hudson's Bay Company in 1670, British fur trade was initiated in the lands served by waters flowing into Hudson Bay, and a permanent trading post was established at Churchill in 1688.

The Hudson's Bay Company was to play a major role in the European exploration of the Keewatin District. In 1761/62, Captain William Christopher of the Hudson's Bay Company became the first European to sail up Chesterfield Inlet as far as the lake where the Thelon, Dubawnt, and Kazan Rivers drain to form the widening of water that the Inuit call "Qamanittuaq" ("place where the river widens"). Christopher assigned the name, "Baker Lake", to this body of water in honour of Sir William Baker, Governor of the Hudson's Bay Company from 1760 to 1770, and his brother, Richard Baker. In the two ensuing centuries and particularly during the past 40 years, Baker Lake or Qamanittuaq,[1] has become a site not just of the meeting of the Keewatin rivers but a site for the meeting of people, ideas, and cultures as well.[2]

Early overland explorations through the Keewatin area were undertaken by Samuel Hearne of the Hudson's Bay Company who reached the Arctic coast at Coppermine in 1771 and by Captain George Back who in 1833 made the first descent of the river which now bears his name.[3] Back encountered a few small groups of Inuit living inland along the Back River and wrote in his journal of his effort "to make them comprehend that we were ... Europeans come to benefit not to injure them."[4]

Contacts between Inuit in the Keewatin District and Europeans accelerated in the 19th century, primarily as a result of Britain's renewed efforts to discover the Northwest Passage.[5] A number of celebrated voyages proved unsuccessful in discovering this desired trade route to India but did extend mapping of the Arctic coast and fostered further contact between Europeans and Inuit. Among the most noted and tragic of the 19th-century explorations was John Franklin's fateful expedition in 1845-48. A seasoned Arctic explorer, Franklin and 128 officers and crew left England on the vessels *Erebus* and *Terror* in 1845, never to be heard from again. The disappearance of the Franklin party prompted more than 50 search expeditions which not only accumulated clues regarding Franklin's demise but added to the knowledge that Europeans and Euro-North Americans had of the Arctic itself.[6] Particularly notable in expanding knowledge about the inland areas of the Central Arctic and in fostering further contact between Inuit of this area and outsiders were search expeditions in the northern Keewatin led by Dr. John Rae of the Hudson's Bay Company in the 1850s and by Americans, Charles Francis Hall in the 1860s and Lieutenant Frederick Schwatka in 1878-80. These search expeditions resulted in further mapping of the Keewatin and in further encounters between Europeans, Euro-North Americans, and Inuit.

After Britain transferred its North American Arctic lands to Canada in 1870, the newly confederated Canadian government undertook its own northern expeditions to advance scientific investigation and to assert sovereignty. The Canadian Geological Survey was initiated with an exploratory voyage to Chesterfield Inlet in 1884. Survey geologists J.B. and J.W. Tyrell traveled extensively inland, west of Hudson Bay, exploring the Dubawnt and Kazan Rivers, Aberdeen Lake, Schultz Lake, and Baker Lake in 1899 and 1901-02. While many of these early explorers and scientists had contact with Inuit, such interaction was sporadic and, for the most part, superficial.

Whaling and trading activities along the coast of Hudson Bay in the late 1800s, had considerable effect on the Inuit in the area. Scottish and American whalers became an almost constant presence along the western coast of Hudson Bay from 1860 to the early 1900s, particularly in the Roes Welcome Sound area which was the primary bowhead whaling theatre of Hudson Bay. Many Inuit living along the coast and inland along the Chesterfield Inlet as far west as Qamanittuaq had significant and sustained interaction with these whalers. Some worked as guides and harpooners during the summer whaling season and settled near the shore stations established at Marble Island and Depot Island during the winter months. Intermarriage and a growing dependence on imported goods such as rifles and ammunition profoundly affected the lives and living patterns of Inuit along the coast and had an impact on the more isolated inland Inuit who became acquainted with Western goods through trade with their coastal neighbours.

The decline of bowhead whaling in Hudson Bay early in the 20th century owing to the declining market for baleen and sperm whale oil coincided with increasingly aggressive efforts on the part of the Hudson's Bay Company to establish an Arctic fur trade.

By the beginning of the 20th century, the market value of white fox had risen to such a level that the operation of permanent Arctic trading posts had become commercially viable. The first Keewatin area Hudson's Bay Company post was established at Chesterfield Inlet in 1911. Other Hudson's Bay posts in the Keewatin quickly followed, as did posts of competing European and Canadian traders.

Qamanittuaq became an active site for the new trading posts. From 1916 to 1926, the Hudson's Bay Company operated a trading post on Okpiktooyuk ("Big Hips Island") on the south side of the lake near the mouth of the Kazan River; a new Hudson's Bay Company post was established at its present site on the west shore of the lake in 1925. Lamson-Hubbard, a Canadian fur-trading company, ran a post on the narrows at the east end of the lake from 1920 until the company was absorbed by the Hudson's Bay Company in 1922. The Bay's longest-standing competitor – the French company, Révillon Frères – operated a trading post at Qamanittuaq from 1924 until it too was bought out by the Hudson's Bay Company in 1936.

The impact of trading posts in the area of Qamanittuaq permanently altered both the technology and the hunting patterns of the Inuit of the Keewatin District and had profound impact on the spiritual culture of the Inuit as well. The introduction of firearms and the concept of trapping for the purpose of trade eroded ethical and spiritual aspects of the traditional hunting culture. While the new technology improved the efficiency of Inuit hunters, it disrupted their relationship with the animals they hunted. No longer was their success in hunting linked to ritualized respect expressed toward the souls and bodies of the animals who they believed willingly sacrificed themselves for the survival of the people.

The spiritual and intellectual culture of the Inuit was also affected by activities of missionaries who sought converts to Christianity throughout the Keewatin. Roman Catholic and Anglican missionaries moved into the Central Arctic by the first decades of this century. The first mission in this area was the Roman Catholic mission established at Chesterfield Inlet in 1912. The Anglican and Roman Catholic Churches established mission posts at Qamanittuaq in 1926 and 1927 respectively, and missionaries of both faiths traveled widely to evangelize Inuit in isolated camps.

The federal government also became a presence early in this century. In 1903 the first permanent Royal Canadian Mounted Police (RCMP) post was established at Cape Fullerton north of Churchill, and regular patrols were made from there to various points along the coast and into Chesterfield Inlet. A temporary RCMP detachment was maintained at the east end of Qamanittuaq from 1915 to 1918 and was reactivated from 1931 to 1936. The present RCMP post on the west end of the lake has been continuously occupied since 1938.

In 1946, Baker Lake was also used as a base for the Canadian Army's Arctic military exercise, "Operation Muskox." In connection with this manoeuvre, the Royal Canadian Air Force built the present 1,220 metre landing strip. Armand Tagoona (No. 35), son of an Inuk mother and German father, was a young man and one of the few permanent residents at the time of Operation Muskox. He recalled how strange this intrusion seemed to the native people.

> I remember ... when DC3 airplanes started to come to Baker Lake, in the year 1946. It was early spring when they landed on the Baker Lake ice, just in front of the settlement.... To us it was a time of wonder and amazement. The next day these two big machines pushed up a pile of snow on the lake, to make a long runway for the airplanes that were to land in the following days.... [T]hen airplanes came and went from Churchill, bringing in drums of gas, two or three times a day. We were wondering what was going on, then we heard rumours that war, the big fight, might be started any time by the Russians. It was an exciting time for us all and we were a little scared at the same time. We just wanted to watch all the airplanes landing and taking off. Then in the spring lots of army men came to Baker Lake and put up their tents where the land air strip is now. They made a lot of noise, day and night, with the two big machines that came from Churchill during the winter. And they scraped the land slowly. When we got near their tents, we heard them talking and laughing. So we never got inside their tents, because they were like animals, jumping up and down, laughing and shouting, and jumping and swimming in the lake where we got our drinking water, and they also washed their bodies in the lake.[7]

In connection with Operation Muskox, the Royal Canadian Signal Corps established a weather station at Baker Lake in 1947. These facilities have been operated since 1948 by the Meteorological Branch of the Federal Department of Transport.

During the early decades of the 20th century, while trading posts, missions, and government installations were being established at Qamanittuaq, the majority of Inuit continued to live in isolated, semi-nomadic hunting camps. Though annual or biennial treks to the trading posts were common for able young men, not all Inuit living in the "old ways" on the land were able to or interested in visiting the posts at such regular intervals. Most remained essentially self-sufficient on the land and isolated from the changes that were occurring in the immediate vicinity of the trading posts.

Outside the Keewatin itself, very little was known about the daily life experience of the Inuit before the early 1920s when a team of Danish scientists, under the leadership of ethnologist, Knud Rasmussen, traveled through this area on a three-year research expedition, the Fifth Thule Expedition. Under the aegis of the Danish Government, Knud Rasmussen and his Danish colleagues, Kaj Birket-Smith, Helge Bangsted, and native Greenlander Qâvigarssuaq, traveled by dog team across the North American Arctic in 1921/24. Rasmussen's reports include detailed observations about the material culture of the Keewatin Inuit and also numerous first-person accounts, songs, and stories that he collected from the Inuit they visited. Based on variations in material culture, hunting patterns, dialect, and other criteria, Rasmussen and his colleagues identified distinct regional groups in the Central Arctic, three of which form the ancestral basis for the current population of Qamanittuaq: (1) Netsilik Inuit who occupied the inland area north of Qamanittuaq and the coastal area around Chantrey Inlet; (2) Caribou Inuit who lived along the Chesterfield Inlet and south of Qamanittuaq; and (3) Iglulik Inuit who lived in the coastal area along the Melville Peninsula and north Baffin Island.[8]

Within each of the regional groups were identifiable subgroups, each associated with a particular hunting area and characterized by distinctive patterns of living and distinctive dialect. In 1922, Rasmussen and Birket-Smith differentiated three subgroups of the inland-dwelling Caribou Inuit: Qainigmiut[9], residing along Chesterfield Inlet and in the area immediately around Baker Lake; Havauqtormiut, living to the south in scattered camps along the lower Kazan River; and Padleimiut, dwelling yet further south on the Kazan River near the Yathkyed and Ennadai Lakes. The latter two were extremely isolated and remained inland throughout the year. The Qainigmiut, however, had a history of contact with Europeans and regularly moved to the coast for the summer. Thus, it was primarily the Qainigmiut and coastal-dwelling Aivilingmiut (a subgroup of the Iglulik Inuit) who were hired by the whalers as boatmen and hunters. Consequently, the Qainigmiut and the Aivilingmiut had relatively greater acquaintance with rifles, tools, and other manufactured goods than did their more isolated inland neighbors. The rifles and canoes they secured in trade enabled them to move further from shore extending their hunting area, and they frequently hunted seal and walrus on the open water. Unlike the coastal Aivilingmiut, the Qainigmiut returned inland to the area around Qamanittuaq for the autumn caribou migrations and to reside for the winter months.

North of Baker Lake were other inland-dwellers. In 1923, Rasmussen became the first ethnographer to visit the inland-dwelling Uqusiksilingmiut ("people of the stone for cooking pots") in the Back River delta.[10] Among the least known and most isolated of all the Inuit at the time of Rasmussen's visit, the Uqusiksilingmiut were perceived by neighbouring Inuit as having an impoverished material culture. Being inland people, they had no seal oil for their lamps and no fuel for fires, and their diet was comprised almost exclusively of fish in the summer and caribou or muskox in the winter. The Copper Inuit, their trade neighbors to the west, described them as "cold and miserable in the extreme"[11] Rasmussen, however, recalled the Uqusiksilingmiut as "the most handsome, elegant and hospitable people (he) met on that long journey; indeed, the healthiest and happiest (he) ever lived with."[12] In the report on his 1923 visit, Rasmussen noted that the Uqusiksilingmiut had been coastal people until the preceding generation when they were introduced to trade goods and abandoned sea mammal hunting for trapping and trading.

> *...they maintained their connection with the sea right down to the last generation and it was only the establishment of the trading post at Baker Lake that induced them to turn to fox trapping and trading and entirely abandon sealing. It is no more than about fifteen years since an Eskimo trader from the (Qainigmiut) ... came right down to Adelaide Peninsula with a sledge loaded with trade goods; he introduced the first guns and the first modern tools. From that time they turned their backs on the sea and adapted themselves entirely to trading, either directly with the white men or with their Eskimo representatives, who sometimes made long journeys for the purpose.[13]*

Relationships among members of the various cultural subgroups of the Keewatin were also noted by long-time Keewatin resident and art collector, Robert Williamson, who described interactions among the groups as "characterized by a form of ethnocentric reserve."[14] Prior to the federal government's establishment of Arctic settlements in the 1950s, contact between cultural subgroups was generally limited to chance encounters or to formalized gatherings for a specific purpose such as trade. Rasmussen described "trade fairs" at Akilineq in the central Keewatin area around Aberdeen Lake where Inuit from all regions of the Keewatin would meet to barter for native copper and soapstone and, later, for iron, wood, and goods received from Europeans or salvaged from abandoned European vessels.[15]

The Settlement of Baker Lake after 1950

When fur prices dropped due to a declining demand for fur garments in Europe during World War II and when the caribou herds entered a cyclical decline during the 1950s, the inland people of the Keewatin were particularly vulnerable. No longer were they able to secure the trade goods on which they had become dependent, and subsistence hunting was extremely difficult. Starvation and disease devastated many camps, killing many, weakening survivors, and putting the well-being of the entire population in jeopardy. To provide immediate and efficient response to these multi-faceted problems, the federal government established centers for medical, educational, and social services in proximity to Arctic trading posts. Inuit who were starving and ill were encouraged to settle near these new facilities.

Before 1950, only a few Inuit families lived in the immediate vicinity of Qamanittuaq, most working as assistants to the traders and missionaries. During the 1950s, however, Qamanittuaq grew to become a permanent community of nearly 400 individuals, more than 90% of whom were relocated Inuit.[16] The Department of National Health and Welfare built a four-room nursing station at Baker Lake in 1950, and the Department of Indian and Northern Affairs assigned a Northern Service Officer to the community in 1956. A federal day school was established in 1957, and pre-fabricated government subsidized housing was constructed from the mid-1950s onward.

For the Inuit, this was a period of profound change. Not only did the relocated Inuit encounter technology, goods, and customs alien to their traditional experience, but they were immersed, for the first time, in a settled community with a large number of people living in proximity to one another. For them, the experience of day-to-day contact with officials and advisors from Southern Canada may have been only slightly more unsettling than the day-to-day contact with Inuit from outside their own family or regional subgroups. During the period of resettlement and even today, extended family units and regional subgroups have served as strong points of identification for Baker Lake Inuit. Robert Williamson investigated intergroup attitudes during the 1960s and discovered a widely-accepted hierarchy among these groups.

> ... among the Keewatin Eskimo, there has long been a sense of hierarchy, a value judgment concerning the intelligence, emotional balance, industriousness, and general competence of the various sub-groups. In this the Aivilingmiut of the north-east corner of the Keewatin have tended to place themselves at the top, and the Qainigmiut next, with the Padleimiut the least respected, particularly those of the deep southern inland plain on the edge of the tree line. Until quite recently, the Back River people remained very remote and usually out of contact with the other Keewatin Eskimo for long periods, but generally, the Uqusiksilingmiut would be rated by the Aivilingmiut as "slightly less than equal" to the Qainigmiut but certainly "superior" to the Padleimiut. It is interesting to note that most of the members of the other groups accept this relative rating, as a value judgement.[17]

Differences in regional dialects, customs, and differential participation in community affairs reinforce the continued distinction among cultural subgroups to the present day.

The population of Baker Lake today is just over 1,200, of whom 90% are Inuit. These Inuit are affiliated with at least ten identifiable cultural subgroups which still form the primary units of their social and cultural identification.[18] Four of these subgroups, which derive ancestral identity from the Netsilik Inuit, comprise the largest population segment in Baker Lake. These subgroups include: (1) Uqusiksilingmiut from the Back River; (2) their neighbors from the West, the Ualingmiut; (3) the Saningayukmiut from Garry Lake; and (4) the Iluiliaqmiut from the coastal area around Gjoa Haven. These four groups[19] share common Netsilik cultural roots and are identifiable by distinctive dialects, customs, and styles of dress.

The next largest segment of the Baker Lake population is comprised of five subgroups whose heritage derives from the inland Caribou Inuit. These include: (1) Qainigmiut, who originally lived along the Chesterfield Inlet as far inland as Qamanittuaq; (2) the Akiliniaqmiut, from Aberdeen Lake west of Qamanittuaq; (3) the Havauqtormiut, who originated in the Lower Kazan River south of Qamanittuaq; (4) the Tariaqmiut, who originally resided along the Hudson Bay coast between Repulse Bay and Arviat; and

(5) a few Padleimiut from the most southerly area of the Upper Kazan River. Also represented in Baker Lake, but in relatively small numbers, are the Aivilingmiut from the Repulse Bay area whose ancestral ties are with the Iglulik Eskimos.

Both the Qaignigmiut and the Aivilingmiut had a long history of interaction with whalers, traders, and missionaries prior to the settlement of Baker Lake. Because of their familiarity with Western ways and their historic proximity to the new settlement, they, along with the nearby Akiliniaqmiut from Aberdeen Lake, became the first to assume wage jobs and positions of responsibility in the new community. The early assumption of influential roles by Inuit in these groups assured them a favoured position *vis-à-vis* Inuit who came into the settlement later. The leadership of the Qaignigmiut, Aivilingmiut, and Akiliniaqmiut in the developing settlement tended to reinforce the pre-existing intergroup evaluations recognized by Williamson. Because Back River and Kazan River Inuit were the last to settle in the community and had come from such isolated areas and in a weakened condition, they were considered by the earlier settlers to be "backward" in dress and custom and deficient in their ability to participate in settlement affairs.

By the time the Back River and Kazan River people settled in Baker Lake, most of the wage jobs and leadership-training positions were already occupied by the earlier residents. In addition, earlier residents in positions of authority tended to grant favors advantaging those with whom they shared familial ties or subgroup affiliation. This exacerbated tensions with the subgroups disadvantaged by such actions. Joanne Bryers' assertion that the Back River people "were habitually considered by other groups as the 'hillbillies,' the savages from the northern barrens, or the untouchables who were not fit for human association"[20] may overstate the prejudice encountered by the Back River people during their early years in Baker Lake. However, the tension among groups – while diminishing - has been a significant factor in the development of the Baker Lake community.

Religious institutions also contributed to reinforcing regional affiliations. Energetic proselytizing by both Roman Catholic and Anglican missionaries during the 1930s and 1940s led most Keewatin Inuit to align themselves with one of these churches, usually the first one to undertake missionary work in their area. Therefore, church affiliation has reinforced regional identification. Inter-marriage between members of different religious denominations is still uncommon. During recent years, additional religious groups have established themselves at Baker Lake. One, the Arctic Christian Fellowship organized in 1971 by Reverend Armand Tagoona, emphasized Inuit cultural heritage and aimed, in part, at reducing divisiveness within the community.

An awareness of the historic divisiveness among subgroups in this community is important, however, in understanding Baker Lake graphic arts. The strident energy and untrammeled vitality of much of Baker Lake's graphic imagery asserts an independence of artistic spirit and an almost startling resistance to externally-imposed standards. Among Western viewers, a frequent first reaction to Baker Lake graphic art compared with graphic art of other Inuit communities is that Baker Lake work is "tougher," "rougher," "more assertive," and more "insistently inventive" than is the gentler, more lyrical work of other Inuit communities such as Cape Dorset or Pangnirtung. The tension in Baker Lake art seems to replicate the tension in the community. No other community in Arctic Canada has been settled from such a vast geographic area or from such a diversity of regional subgroups. In light of the intensity of regional identification among inhabitants of the community – particularly in the early settlement period – this is a dynamic that cannot be overlooked in seeking an understanding for Baker Lake graphic art.

Arts and Crafts Projects in Qamanittuaq

It was in the general context of dislocation and disparate regional allegiances that arts and crafts activities were introduced in Qamanittuaq in the 1960s. Initial efforts to establish arts and crafts programs were undertaken during the winter of 1961-62 when experienced crafts officer, William Larmour, of the Department of Indian Affairs and Northern Development was sent to the community to explore the potential for developing projects similar to those which had proved so successful at Cape Dorset and in Nunavik (Arctic Québec). Indications of artistic potential among the Keewatin Inuit had been reported earlier to both the Canadian Handicraft Guild [21] and to the federal government.

As early as 1947, Major J. D. Cleghorn had informed the Canadian Handicraft Guild of carvings he had seen while participating in the Army's Operation Muskox manoeuvre and had suggested that the Keewatin Inuit should be encouraged in this activity.[22]

That same year, Colonel P. D. Baird, Commander of Operation Muskox, worked with the Canadian Handicraft Guild to contact all white women residing in the Keewatin, urging them to "gather around them neighbouring Eskimo men and women and encourage basket weaving, parka sewing, carving, etc."[23] By 1957, Northern Services Officer Doug Wilkinson encouraged the development of an arts and craft industry in Baker Lake,[24] and in 1960, Edith Dodds, wife of the new Northern Service Officer, initiated an informal handicraft program among women in the settlement.

When Larmour arrived in Baker Lake in November, 1961, there was a readiness among the economically depressed Inuit to participate in the art projects; this was particularly true among the most severely depressed people from the Back River and Kazan River areas, primarily Uqusiksilingmiut and Havauqtormiut. When the Back River and Kazan River people first moved to Baker Lake, some aspects of their lives remained much as they had been on the land. There was very little government housing in the new settlement prior to the mid-1960s, and the relocated Inuit continued to live in tents in the warmer months and snow houses in the wintertime. However, health care and government subsidy for food, clothing, fuel, and other supplies which could be purchased through the Hudson's Bay Company materially improved their lives and reduced the immediate risk of starvation.

With the increased dependence on trade goods, however, came the transition from a subsistence economy based on hunting to a cash economy. Sporadic trade with the Hudson's Bay Company during the years prior to relocation had provided some experience with an abstract medium of exchange. However, there were significant differences between the old trade practices and the new cash economy.[25] Primary among these differences was the fact that the "purchasing power" of an individual was no longer exclusively linked to success in the culturally valued activities of hunting and trapping. Rather, in the new scheme, the amount of money a person was able to control established a person's position in the social and economic structure of the new community. Money became not just a medium of exchange but a measure of status and personal merit. Therefore, the Uqusiksilingmiut and Havauqtormiut were not only materially disadvantaged but their lack of gainful employment and their relative poverty caused them to be socially devalued in the new community. It was primarily the successful participation of these newcomers in the art projects that led to a reversal of this view and helped to mitigate some of the psychological and economic problems that might otherwise have demoralized and isolated the Uqusiksilingmiut and Havauqtormiut.

The Uqusiksilingmiut, particularly, became actively involved in the new art projects. Of the 19 artists in this exhibition, ten are Uqusiksilingmiut from the Back River, Chantrey Inlet and Garry Lake areas north of Baker Lake. All ten moved into the settlement within a four year period around 1960 when life on the land was particularly harsh. Declining caribou herds and disease led to the death of a number of their relatives and jeopardized their survival. Two among these (Oonark and Anguhadluq) were among the first to embrace the opportunity to make drawings when graphic arts projects started. All of Oonark's eight surviving children have also become artists; four represented in this exhibition are Janet Kigusiuq, Victoria Mamnguqsualuk, Nancy Pukingrnak, and William Noah. Anguhadluq's wife, Marion Tuu'luuq, and daughter, Ruth Qualluaryuk, and his adopted son, Mark Uqayuittuq, are also among the Uqusiksilingmiut artists as is Simon Tookoome who came originally from Gjoa Haven. Other artists from Netsilik group include Hannah Kigusiuq, who is Uqusiksilingmiut from Garry Lake, and Harold Qarliqsaq whose background was a mix of Ualingmiut and Iluiliagmiut.

Other artists were relatively evenly split between the Havauqtormiut from the Kazan River area and the Qainigmiut who had lived in the vicinity of Baker Lake. Irene Avaalaaqiaq is Havauqtormiut from the Kazan River area, as was Martha Ittuluka'naaq.

Myra Kukiiyaut and Ruth Annaqtuusi Tulurialik are Qainigmiut and have lived most of their lives in the vicinity of Baker Lake. Armand Tagoona came from Repulse Bay and had a mixed Inuit/European background; his mother was Aivilingmiut and his father was German. Françoise Oklaga moved to Baker Lake only in 1975 from Chesterfield Inlet, though she was adopted as an infant from an Inuit family from south Baffin Island.

In the early 1960s when William Larmour explored the possibility of establishing a graphic arts program in Qamanittuaq, the recently relocated people were among the first to respond to requests for drawings. Pencil drawings by Oonark, Anguhadluq and others convinced Larmour of the potential for a graphic arts program in Baker Lake. It was not until 1963, however, that a formal arts program was actually instituted in Baker Lake and not until 1970 that the graphics component became a reality.

Gabriel Gély became Baker Lake's first official resident craft officer in 1963. An artist with facility in Inuktitut, Gély had worked for several years as a cook with the Department of Transport in various Arctic sites including Ennadai Lake in the southern Keewatin District. Because he was already known to some Baker Lake Inuit, (particularly the Havauqtormiut and Padliemiut who had resided near Ennadai Lake) his efforts to introduce soapstone sculpture, sewing projects, caribou hoof jewelry, and tapestry were quickly accepted by these groups. A number of experimental stonecut prints were attempted with Gély's guidance during his two year residence in Baker Lake, but the results "were not considered promising"[26] and did not lead to editions of salable prints. When Gély departed in February 1965, he was followed during the remaining years of the 1960s by a succession of crafts officers, all of whom made personal contributions to the community but none of whom remained with the Craft Shop long enough to sustain a graphic arts program. Gély's immediate successor was Roderick McCarthy who spent several months during 1965 in Baker Lake guiding local stonecarvers in the techniques of carving and inking stone blocks for the production of stonecut prints. The resulting collection of proofs was submitted to the Canadian Eskimo Art Committee[27] and received the Committee's enthusiastic approval in August of 1965. Unfortunately, ill health forced McCarthy's untimely withdrawal from Baker Lake before the stonecut prints could be editioned. In an attempt to salvage these initial printmaking efforts, the Department of Indian Affairs and Northern Development contracted Robert Paterson, a Toronto printmaker with previous experience at Cape Dorset, to spend ten weeks in Baker Lake assisting the printers in completing the editions. When Paterson arrived in Baker Lake in November, he discovered that "most of the stone blocks had been ground down, and work had to begin again. There was no suitable stone available, and Paterson used the short time remaining to teach linocut techniques."[28] The complications in producing the 1965 prints resulted in a temporary suspension of the Baker Lake printmaking program.

In April 1966, a new craft officer was appointed to Baker Lake – Boris Kotelowitz, a Toronto-trained sculptor/designer who had previously assisted Gabriel Gély in developing the Eskimo Gallery of the National Museum of Man in Ottawa. Kotelowitz established an immediate rapport with the older people in the community and played an active role in encouraging local carving and securing new local sources of good soapstone. Charged also with re-establishing the printmaking program, Kotelowitz resumed the practice of purchasing drawings and initiated further experimentation with printmaking. Reflecting later on the Baker Lake printmaking experience of the late 1960s, Kotelowitz explained that the production of high quality prints was a slow and difficult undertaking in Baker Lake because of the initial inadequacy of studio facilities and because of the developmental time necessary for untrained stonecarvers to acquire facility with the newly-introduced printmaking techniques.[29] When Kotelowitz resigned in the spring of 1969, the Department of Indian Affairs and Northern Development appointed Ken Krassweller to carry forward the printmaking efforts. Under Krassweller's guidance earlier linocut images were transferred to stone but the results were unsuccessful, and printmaking was again temporarily suspended.

The printmaking program was revived again the summer of 1969, however, and this time with striking success. George Swinton, artist and noted writer on Inuit art, recommended the appointment of two American artists – Sheila and Jack Butler. In July 1969, the Butlers arrived in Qamanittuaq and enthusiastically initiated efforts to re-establish local interest in the graphic arts. The Butlers reorganized the printshop and began the execution of prints using drawings collected by previous craft officers. They also renewed a vigorous program of purchasing drawings and offered an hourly wage to Inuit willing to learn printmaking by assisting in the printshop. The response to the Butlers' efforts was immediate. By November 1969, a portfolio of 31 proof prints was ready for review by the Canadian Eskimo Arts Council, and in the spring of 1970, the first annual Baker Lake print collection was launched in an exhibition at the Edmonton Art Gallery. From the outset, the Butlers emphasized collaboration and local management and provided primarily technical advice. The 1970 print collection and those that followed represented an inventive blending of ideas and technologies, creating (as Peter Millard points out in his essay in this catalogue) a new hybrid artistic expression.

The Baker Lake graphic arts program flourished during the early-1970s. With the Butlers' encouragement, Inuit artists quickly assumed leadership responsibility for the activities of the printshop. Three Uqusiksilingmiut elders (Oonark, Anguhadluq, and Tuu'luuq) became mainstays in creating images to support the printmaking program when it was put on a successful footing in the early 1970s. Oonark and Anguhadluq alone, in their 60s and 70s respectively, were responsible for nearly half of the print images produced during the time of the Butlers' residency and consultancy to the Baker Lake printshop. Together, Oonark and Anguhadluq produced the original drawings for 95 of the 229 Baker Lake prints produced between 1970 and 1976.

In 1971, with the Butlers' guidance and a $50,000 loan from the federal Eskimo Loan Fund, a cooperative called Sanavik (meaning "work place") was established in Qamanittuaq to foster and coordinate the art activities in the settlement. In 1972, after two-and-a-half years in Baker Lake, the Butlers resigned and left the community, though they continued as consultants until 1976. With periodic visits from the Butlers, Inuit artists carried forward the printmaking program and issued well-received annual collections of stonecut and stencil prints. When the Butlers formally resigned in 1976, the Sanavik printmakers attempted to carry on without external assistance. However, they missed the technical guidance and external advice, and, in the summer of 1977, appointed John Evans as art advisor to the Co-op.

A tragic fire in December 1977 leveled the Sanavik Co-op building, destroying not only the 1978 print collection which was in production at the time but also the print stones and all the original drawings stored at the Co-op. Various governmental departments and other agencies helped to restore material losses, and Evans and the artists and printmakers of Baker Lake worked vigorously to create and print new images for a 1978 print collection. Because of time constraints and the unavailability of a sufficient supply of good quality soapstone, linocuts were again introduced.

When Evans left Baker Lake in 1979, he was replaced by Toronto-trained printmaker, Bogus Zydb, who served as arts advisor to the Sanavik Co-operative from mid-1979 until late-1982. Economic recession in the early-1980s weakened the North American art market, however, diminishing print sales and deflating both the economic base and the morale at the Co-op. In 1983, for the first time since 1970, Baker Lake did not issue an annual print collection.

By late 1983, modest economic recovery had begun, and artist/photographer William Eakin replaced Zydb as arts advisor to Sanavik. Under Eakin's guidance, a combined 1983/84 print collection was released as well as an annual collection for 1985. When Eakin left Baker Lake in early-1985, he was replaced by Winnipeg art historian and curator, Grace Eiko Thomson, who remained with the Sanavik Co-op as arts advisor through 1988. Following the dissolution of the Canadian Eskimo Arts Council in 1989, the Inuit artists and printmakers of Baker Lake decided to move forward in the production of an annual print collection without the benefit of an arts advisor from outside the community. Overcoming severe economic setbacks and organizational challenges which delayed the print collection an entire year, members of the Sanavik Co-op completed their first independently produced print collection in 1990. Technical problems, however, along with continuing financial instability and competing agendas for the Co-op resulted in an indefinite suspension of the printmaking program after 1990.

Many of the artists of Qamanittuaq continue to draw despite the termination of the printmaking program, and the distribution of their drawings is facilitated today by Euro-Canadian dealers and private entrepreneurs both in Baker Lake and elsewhere. However, as William Noah points out in his essay in this catalogue, the future for art projects in Baker Lake is unclear. Directions such projects take will inevitably reflect the multiplicity of influences which, like a river widening and absorbing smaller streams, continues to shape the dynamic of Qamanittuaq.

Notes

1. In this essay, the Inuktitut term, "Qamanittuaq," will be used interchangeably with Baker Lake. Both terms refer to the widening of water called "Baker Lake" by William Christopher and to the settlement of "Baker Lake" which is known in Inuktitut as "Qamanittuaq."

2. Much of the information of this essay is drawn from my doctoral research undertaken in Baker Lake during the early 1980s. For a complete account of this research, see Marion E. Jackson, "Baker Lake Inuit Drawings: A Study in the Evolution of Artistic Self-Consciousness" (Ph.D. diss., Ann Arbor: University of Michigan, 1985).

3. This river was previously known by its Chipewyan name, *Thlew-ee-choh*, meaning "Great Fish River."

4. George Back, *Narrative of the Arctic Land Expedition to the Mouth of the Great Fish River and Along the Shores of the Arctic Ocean, in the Years 1833, 1834, and 1835* (London: John Murray, 1836); 2nd ed. (Philadelphia: E.L. Carey & A. Hart, 1937), p. 287.

5. A number of voyages to discover the Northwest Passage were initiated by the British in the late 16th and early 17th centuries. Voyages by Martin Frobisher, John Davis, Henry Hudson, Robert Bylot, and Luke Foxe were among the most celebrated. After the early 17th century, such voyages were virtually discontinued until the early 19th century. For a comprehensive account of 19th-century exploration seeking the Northwest Passage, see Pierre Berton, *The Arctic Grail: The Quest for the Northwest Passage and the North Pole 1818-1909* (Toronto: McClelland and Stewart, 1988).

6. For a full account of Franklin's expedition and the search expeditions that followed, see Berton, pp. 150-408.

7. Armand Tagoona, *Shadows* (Ottawa: Oberon Press, 1975), opposite Plate 8.

8. The English translations of Rasmussen's reports of the Fifth Thule Expedition use the terms "Netsilik Eskimos," "Caribou Eskimos," and "Iglulik Eskimos" to identify these groups. However, current practice is to use the Inuktitut term, "Inuit," rather than "Eskimo" in referring to the native inhabitants of the Arctic. I have followed current practice throughout this essay. For Rasmussen's descriptions of these regional groups, see Knud Rasmussen, *The Intellectual Culture of the Iglulik Eskimos*, Report of the Fifth Thule Expedition, 1921-1924, vol 7, no. 1, W.E. Calvert trans. (Copenhagen: Glydendalske Boghandel, Nordisk Forlag, 1930); Knud Rasmussen, *Observations on the Intellectual Culture of the Caribou Eskimos*, Report of the Fifth Thule Expedition, 1921- 1924, vol 7, no. 2, W.E. Calvert trans. (Copenhagen: Glydendalske Boghandel, Nordisk Forlag, 1931); and Knud Rasmussen, *The Netsilik Eskimos: Social Life and Spiritual Culture*, Report of the Fifth Thule Expedition, 1921-1924, vol 8, no. 2, W.E. Calvert trans. (Copenhagen: Glydendalske Boghandel, Nordisk Forlag, 1931).

9. Rasmussen was son of a native Greenlandic mother and a Danish father, and he spoke Inuktitut as well as Danish. On the Fifth Thule Expedition, he recorded the Inuktitut names of the regional Inuit groups as these names were given to him by the Inuit. Ramussen used phonetic transcriptions to record these group names. In more recent literature, many of Rasmussen's original spellings have been replaced by spellings which reflect an attempt to achieve a consistent orthography for recording the Inuktitut language. To avoid the confusion of differing spellings in this essay, I have adopted the currently accepted spelling of the names of the regional subgroups. The following spellings are used in this essay. Among the Caribou Inuit: Qainigmiut (Rasmussen's Qaernermiut); Havauqtormiut (Rasmussen's Havaqtômiut); Padleimiut (Rasmussen's Pâdlermiut); Akiliniaqmiut and Tariaqmiut. Among the Iglulik Inuit: Aivilingmiut (Rasmussen's Aivilimiut). Among the Netsilik Inuit: Uqusiksilingmiut (Rasmussen's Utkuhikjalingmiut); Ualingmiut (Rasmussen's Hailingnayokmiut); Saningayukmiut and Iluiliaqmiut.

10. For Rasmussen's observations on the Uqusiksilingmiut, see Rasmussen, *The Netsilik Eskimos*, pp. 457-542.

11. Diamond Jenness, *Life of the Copper Eskimos*, Report of the Canadian Arctic Expedition 1913-1918, Vol. 12. Ottawa: F.A. Acland for the Department of Naval Service, 1922, p. 101.

12. Rasmussen, *The Netsilik Eskimos*, p. 542.

13. Rasmussen, *The Netsilik Eskimos*, p. 473-474,

14. Robert G. Williamson, "The Keewatin in Settlements," *The Musk Ox*, 8 (1971), p. 17.

15. See Rasmussen, *The Netsilik Eskimos*, p. 481. For additional accounts of trade among Inuit from different regions, also see David Damas, "The Traditional Culture of the Central Eskimos" in *Arctic Life: Challenge to Survive*, Martina Margenau Jacobs and James B. Richardson III, eds. (Pittsburgh: Carnegie Museum of Natural History, Carnegie Institute, 1983), pp. 113-148. Damas has documented the extensive trade patterns that existed in the Central Arctic prior to the influence of European contact. The uneven distribution of natural resources led Copper Netsilik, and Iglulik Eskimos to travel hundreds of kilometres (often over periods extending a year or more) to the Thelon River for trade and to collect driftwood carried by the Thelon from wooded areas further west.

16. F.G. Vallee, *Kabloona and Eskimo in the Central Keewatin* (Ottawa: Saint Paul University, 1967), p. 10.

17. Williamson, p. 17.

18. Information on the cultural subgroups represented in Baker Lake today was attained through personal conversations with various people in Baker Lake during the past several years, particularly William Noah, the late Armand Tagoona, and the Reverend Brian Ford. Without exception, all Inuit with whom I discussed this subject could confidently and accurately identify the specific regional affiliation of others in the community while most whites were unable to do so and many whites were aware only in very general terms of a diversity of regional origins represented in the Baker Lake Inuit population.

19. Jean Briggs identified these same four subgroups in her important study of Back River Inuit undertaken in 1963-65. See Jean L. Briggs, *Never In Anger: Portrait of an Eskimo Family* (Cambridge: Harvard University Press, 1970), p. 12. However, Robert Williamson's sources informed him that the Ualingmiut (Ualiakliit) were not a separate group but a subdivision of the Saningayukmiut. Briggs continued to recognize the four separate groups, as had Rasmussen. All four groups were recognized by Baker Lake Inuit with whom I spoke in 1983 as well.

20. Joanne Elizabeth Bryers, "The Graphic Art of the Baker Lake Eskimos from July 1969 to July 1973." (M.A. thesis, University of Toronto, 1974) p. 46.

21. Originating out of the Women's Art Association which was founded in 1902, the Canadian Handicraft Guild was formed in 1906 as a non-profit organization committed to (1) encouraging, retaining and developing handicrafts in Canada and (2) providing public education regarding the value of arts and crafts. Headquartered in Montreal, the Guild developed branch organizations in major cities across Canada and assumed an active role in encouraging the retention and development of handicrafts among native peoples of Canada. In 1967, the organization officially changed its name to the Canadian Guild of Crafts. For a history of the Guild's role in encouraging contemporary Inuit art, see Virginia Watt, ed., *Canadian Guild of Crafts Québec: The Permanent Collection* (Montreal: Canadian Guild of Crafts, Quebec, 1980).

22. George Swinton, *Sculpture of the Eskimo* (Greenwich, Connecticut: New York Graphic Society, 1972) reprint ed., (Toronto: McClelland and Stewart, 1982) p. 125.

23. Swinton, p. 125.

24. Cynthia Waye Cook, *From the Centre: The Drawings of Luke Anguhadluq.* (Toronto: Art Gallery of Ontario, 1993), p. 6.

25. It was common practice up to the 1950s for Hudson's Bay Company traders to offer as trade tokens small marked blocks of wood of different sizes in exchange for furs. The wooden tokens could be exchanged immediately for trade items such as ammunition, tea, sugar, rifles, canoes, etc. To this day, a colloquial word for "twenty-five cents" in Baker Lake is the Inuktitut translation for "half-block-of-wood."

26. Helga Goetz, *The Inuit Print/L'estampe inuit* (Ottawa: National Museums of Canada, 1976), p. 192.

27. The Canadian Eskimo Arts Committee (renamed the Canadian Eskimo Arts Council in 1967) was established by the federal government in 1961 at the request of northern cooperatives to advise on the artistic merits of annual print collections and, with a blind embossed seal, to certify the authenticity and quality of individual works in the annual print collections. The Canadian Eskimo Arts Council was discontinued in 1989.

28. Bryers, p. 14.

29. Boris Kotelowitz, personal communication, 1983.

BAKER LAKE
DRAWINGS

PETER MILLARD

These extraordinary drawings from Baker Lake present a puzzle to the average Southern viewer. They seem, at the same time, both familiar and strange. They are familiar because they use materials that are traditional in the South and appear, at first glance, to be drawings like any others one would expect to find in an exhibition. They are strange, however, because when we look more closely it appears that their subject matter, and the ways in which that subject matter is presented, are unlike anything we are used to. How, then, should we approach the drawings?

Perhaps it will help if, to begin with, we think through a comment by Hal N. Opperman:

> *Inuit art is the result of a propitious interface between two alien cultures. This kind of interface is nothing new; in fact, it has happened quite frequently in the history of art and has often produced stunning bodies of work which, like that of the Inuit, share qualities and values of both cultures....*[1]

This is a provocative idea: Inuit art as a hybrid. Hybrids are vigorous, and cross-fertilization is essential for progress. Also, very important, the hybrid becomes an individual species, unique to itself. If we accept this notion, it follows that one way to approach the drawings is to try to see them as a form in their own right, somewhat like Southern modes, but not of them. Such a process involves noting the ways in which they differ from Southern forms, and in order to do this it might be useful to remind ourselves what those Southern forms are and the extent to which our way of seeing has been modified by the artistic conventions belonging to our particular culture.

Since the Renaissance, and until the last hundred years or so, Southern artists have been concerned with exploiting two main visual devices in their works: sculptural form and linear perspective. Sculptural form is the technique of shading in order to give to an image the illusion of three-dimensional form, and linear perspective is a complicated technique designed to make objects look as if they are receding in space. Both are methods of achieving three-dimensional verisimilitude on a two-dimensional surface.

It is hardly necessary to point out how triumphantly successful these techniques have been in the hands of the master draughtsmen over, roughly, the past half-millennium. Together, they have left such a glorious and convincing legacy of drawings that we tend to assign a sort of inevitability to this way of seeing. But there is nothing inevitable about it, and it certainly is not the only way to view reality. Daniel Mendelowitz is right when he declares that "As we survey the long vistas of history we see ever-changing beliefs and social institutions shaping the artist's concerns, or, we might say, providing the focus that determined what and how the artist saw."[2]

In other words, drawing, like all other art forms, will be both culture specific and historically specific. Sculptural form and linear perspective, so familiar to us, are not inevitable, but are the result of a particular culture and a particular outlook, reflecting the values of that culture. The technique favours the discrete object; it demands a fixed, single viewpoint appropriate to a society that is striving for a uniform and objective concept of external reality. It is an excellent tool, for instance, for scientific study, which requires a notationally accurate portrayal of objects – it is difficult to imagine how medicine, engineering, architecture, etc., could have developed without it. At the same time, the technique tends to the static; movement can be suggested only by depicting an object caught, as in a photograph, at one point of action. Similarly, the technique is restricted in time; when attempting narrative it can illustrate only one moment. It is an authoritarian technique, and its authoritarianism is reflected in its unforgiving nature – in a traditional drawing even a slight deviation from the rules of linear perspective, for instance, results in an immediately obvious "error."

Sculptural form and linear perspective are, in fact, the code forms of a materialist philosophy best represented by Descartes, for whom "The essence of physical, bodily substance is extension. It occupies space, exists in time, is tangible, visible, locatable, changing, divisible, has shape and can be moved from place to place."[3] The Southern mode is admirably adapted, also, to a culture whose intellectual endeavour is concerned, to a large extent, with analysis and taxonomy – examining things minutely and identifying them as discrete entities.

Such an outlook is foreign to the Inuit consciousness, and one of the rewards of studying the Baker lake drawings is the expansion of our imaginations as we experience a new way of seeing. The drawings might also help us better understand certain elements in modern art. Much of modern art, with its deliberate disruption of traditional techniques, can be seen as a rebellion against what is static and restrictive in Cartesian rationalism. Modern art demanded a new way of seeing, and the basic urge was a desire for artistic freedom, for flexibility, for freshness, and above all, for the chance to start all over again. The art of the past was burdened with too much self-knowledge, leading to a sort of after-the-Fall angst.[4]

It did not really work; no modern artist, of course, trained in the Southern tradition, could cut him or herself totally off from the past. Any re-ordering inevitably implies the thing re-ordered, so that a truly new approach, uncontaminated by the past, cannot be made from within ones own culture. Instead, one needs a people largely ignorant of the history of art or of Southern culture – a people like the Inuit of the Canadian Arctic. For us, part of the fascination of the Baker Lake drawings lies in the fact that they contain the freedom that much modern art strives for, but with no consciousness of that fact. Inuit art seems to go back to the beginning, before the materialism and tendency for disjunction that characterize modern Southern culture.

It is true that by the time of Jack and Sheila Butler's arrival at Baker Lake in 1969, the Inuit there had already had a considerable amount of contact with white people. Even so, we can be sure that none of them had much acquaintance with the history and theory of Southern art, and while the arts and crafts officers did offer tactful guidance, it did not materially affect the artists' vision.[5] When the Butlers handed out paper and pencils to anyone interested, the stage was set for one of the most extraordinary experiments in the history of Canadian art.

For many of the artists this was their first attempt to visualize and objectify their world. With no past examples to guide them, and with only the vaguest idea of what was expected of them, the artists were free to work as the spirit moved them. Drawing, it has often been remarked, is the most direct and intimate of all the art forms, and this personal directness, coupled with the relative freedom from example, resulted in drawings of astonishing freshness and individuality.

However, varied as the drawings are from artist to artist, it is possible to see certain common features that make them different from Southern drawings and which contribute to a sense of what might be called, for want of a better term, their 'Inuitness.' What follows is an attempt to point out some of these features.

There is always a danger of misunderstanding graphic work from another culture. But in the case of the Baker Lake drawings about to be discussed, the danger is lessened by the fact that we have the comments of the artists themselves. In the spring of 1983, the Macdonald Stewart Art Centre arranged for Marion Jackson to take photographs of various drawings to Baker Lake and, with the help of William Noah as translator, to interview the artists about them – with fascinating results.[6]

Two caveats are in order, however. First, what we have to go on is an edited version of a translator's version of what the artist said, so that much intervenes between the artist's words and what was finally printed on the page. Nuances must have been lost. Second, the difference between the aesthetic concepts of the South and those of the Inuit is so great (or was at the time of the interviews) that misunderstanding or lack of connection are almost bound to occur. Allied to this is the problem of differing protocol; not understanding the purpose behind a question, the interviewee is likely to make a somewhat arbitrary response. Indeed, it is not unknown for an artist to give one explanation for a drawing one day, only to offer something quite different another day. Fortunately, however, the fact that explanations may shift somewhat does not affect the essential nature of the drawings.

Using the artists' comments as a guide, we can point out certain characteristics of the Baker Lake drawings that will help us to understand them more clearly and to enjoy them more fully. Because a critical vocabulary for this type of art is virtually non-existent, we must begin constructing one, as with the terms "Syncretism" and "Meta-realism."

Syncretism

The Inuit freedom from the rationalism that haunts Southern art, with its concern with the discrete image, is seen nowhere more clearly than in the lack of regard that the Baker Lake artists have for consistent context, or the nonchalance with which they will introduce a fantastic element into an otherwise literal image. This habit of joining several apparently unconnected elements into one image I have termed Syncretism.

Look, for instance, at Marion Tuu'luuq's drawing based on the Kukiiyuaq legend (No.16). The two images at the top, she tells us: "... are just fish. I sort of decorated them. They have nothing to do with the story."[7] Similarly, Nancy Pukingrnak explains the origin of the faces on the backs of the figures in her strange drawing (No. 70). The drawing is analogous, we learn, to one of her soapstone carvings: "I was making a figure of a person, and the stone had lumps on the back of it, so that's how it turned out to be. By thinking of that same carving, I thought of making these images."[8]

The clearest expression of what I have termed Syncretism, however, is found in the interviews with Jessie Oonark, particularly in her comments on her drawing *Untitled (fish women)* (No. 15). "Those two ladies are chanting and singing," Oonark remarks. "They have a kind of a fish body. It's only a piece of paper, and I just added those fish images onto those ladies there. I just drew this from my mind."[9]

"It's only a piece of paper." The Inuit artist is not on oath when faced with a blank sheet. The trained Southern artist, though, willingly or not, is bound always by a silent and largely unconscious complex of obligations – aesthetic, philosophical, psychological, logical – if only to deny them.

The apparent arbitrariness with which the Baker Lake artists create their images should give pause to Southern viewers who hunger after the magic-religious element that is so lacking in their own lives, and who consequently are eager to see it in the art of other cultures. I suspect that Oonark's *Untitled (fish women)* for instance, has frequently been mistaken for a depiction of the Inuit goddess Sedna. Actually, Sedna, a sea goddess, is not likely to appear in the belief system of the inland people of Baker Lake.

On the other hand, we would probably be right not to take the artists' dismissive statements too literally. Many artists are elusive when pressed about their work, and the Inuit, in particular, are noted for their modesty and self-deprecation. Obviously, there is more going on in these drawings than their comments suggest, perhaps more than the artists themselves realize. The very freedom with which they can approach their work, and the sense of openness before a sheet of paper, are conducive to a state that would allow the subconscious full play. Surrealism in Inuit art generally is a subject that invites investigation.

Meta-realism

Another way in which Inuit art is free of the restrictions accompanying traditional Southern art forms is illustrated in the drawings of Myra Kukiiyaut and Simon Tookoome. Most Southern art privileges what is observable through the senses; Inuit art regards what is not seen as equally real and often puts it into the artwork, a practice that I have termed Meta-realism.

This important principle in Inuit art is illustrated with remarkable vividness by Myra Kukiiyaut's comments on her animal/human group (No. 41). She tells us that the drawing depicts just an ordinary family,

But the man was able to think in order to survive and feed his family.... These animal images are not present but in his mind- sort of a vision that he is able to deduct, knowing the animals are there somewhere. That's why he has two heads – to show that he is an ordinary man but also that he is thinking of these visions."[10]

Now we can understand why the animals are depicted in a schematic way, their immateriality wonderfully suggested by their fluid, wavy treatment.

Of all the Baker Lake artists, it is Simon Tookoome who most consistently employs Meta-realism. His characteristic Picasso-like double profiles are explained by his comments on a drawing not in the exhibition (Fig. 1). It is of a single standing man whose head is made up of two profile faces apparently looking at each other. "This is actually one person who is looking both ways, looking at the animals..." Tookoome explained. This figure is remarkable also for a series of heads, seemingly attached to the sides of his legs. Like the animals in Kukiiyaut's drawing, we learn from Tookoome, they are thought made visible: "On the legs are images of heads that he is thinking of, sort of like he is wishing to see other people."[11] Tookoome's method is made even clearer in his remarks on the drawing *Isumavuq - A Person in Thought* (No. 56).

Any images that you see, especially a face with images of animals on its cheeks, means that the person is thinking of that species of animal, sort of like having a vision, or a daydream of animals.[12]

Multiple Time and Space

The Southern concept of realism demands that narrative be presented in a linear manner. There are exceptions, but the usual expectation is that things happening in different places at different times cannot be shown all at once; rather, they require a series of separate presentations, as in a cartoon strip, or the stations of the cross in a church.

The Inuit artist observes no such convention. An example is Irene Avaalaaqiaq's *Untitled (story of the fish that swallows people)* (No. 64). Avaalaaqiaq's commentary explains that the drawing illustrates the legend of a giant fish that swallowed and eventually disgorged a person who, while inside the fish, turned into a bird or a fish. The lower righthand corner, she tells us, shows the giant fish swallowing its prey; just above that image it is seen disappearing inside; then the lefthand side of the drawing shows the prey emerging.[13]

Fig. 1
Simon Tookoome
Person Who is Looking Both Ways,
1975
coloured pencil on paper
MS980.107

Fig. 2

Victoria Mamnguqsualuk

Untitled (eagle eating humans and animals), 1982

coloured pencil on black paper MS983.001

This habit of collapsing time and space is encouraged, it seems, by the artists' sense of the physicality of the sheet of paper on which they are working, and its size limitation. Victoria Mamnguqsualuk made some very interesting remarks in this regard during an interview about one of her drawings (Fig. 2). Two of the figures, she explained,

are supposed to be behind – way behind or someplace else. Because of the size of the paper, the things seem to be very close. Some things happened at one certain time, and some things at another time, but, because of the size of the paper, you can't really put everything separate."[14]

A common feature of the Baker Lake drawings is multiple perspective. There is no single viewpoint, as in most Southern art, but on the same page figures and objects may be presented from several different angles (No. 4, 21, 33, 7). Such freedom is to be expected, given the Inuit artists' ignorance of the techniques of linear perspective, the sense of limited space on the paper, and their own approach to reality.

A notable feature of the Baker Lake drawings is the absence of portraits of actual people and the scarcity of depictions of a specific landscape. Southern art is full of both. The portrait springs from the Southern cult of individuality, while landscape in art comes from a variety of causes: from an imagined relationship with Nature, either aesthetic, spiritual, or nostalgic, and often, too, from a sense of ownership, in either the literal or emotional sense.

Landscape does appear as a physical reality in the drawings of one or two Baker Lake artists, such as William Noah, or Simon Tookoome, and Luke Anguhadluq's exquisite drawing, *Untitled (dog team)* (No. 1) seems isolated in the whiteness of snow. For the most part, landscape is either absent or is generalized. Similarly, while humans are a major subject in the drawings, they too are generalized, the facial features often stylized as in Byzantine art.

The non-specific nature of the drawings is what one would expect from the characteristics described earlier. Syncretism, meta-realism, and multiple time and space, all are suited to an art which is general rather than particular, and which is symbolic rather than notational.

The absence of linear perspective and volume, aids in the symbolic purpose. As Mendelowitz points out: "Flat, unmodulated surfaces carry as pattern, rather than as form."[15] Pattern is prominent in many of the Baker Lake drawings: pattern is repetition, repetition suggests ritual, and ritual requires symbolism.

Here we arrive at what I take to be the essence of Baker Lake graphics (equally true of the prints and wall hangings). It is largely a symbolic art, collective and celebratory. It is based on a simple interconnection of just three elements: the family, animals and the spirit world. The human family and animals are bound together in a profound relationship that is both physical and mystical, hence the importance of the shaman, whose main function was to mediate between humans and animals.

The relationship is beautifully illustrated in Myra Kukiiyaut's drawing, already mentioned, showing a family caught in a swirling dance of wished-for animals, some of them apparently in spirit form (No. 41). As Kukiiyaut says with deceptive simplicity:

"This is... a man and a woman and a baby and so on.... A man can kill a fish or kill an animal in order to support his family and vice versa. Like after the man kills (and gives the fish or meat to the woman), a woman can sort of work on the meat or cook it and then give it to the man. So they are both giving to each other."[16]

And the animals, she might have added, are giving to the family.

Almost all of the Baker Lake drawings are emblematic to one degree or another, but two artists are pre-eminent for this quality. Luke Anguhadluq's "primitive" and rather scratchy drawings engage us because of their freshness and delicacy, but also because they manage to be both intimate and collective. His depiction of men fishing, for instance, suggests at one and the same time a personal experience and the general activity of fishing (No. 4). The splendid *Drum Dance* (No. 3), is an even more successful image. A drawing with such a dominant pattern risks being static, but in fact the variations in the angle and colour of the dancers create a lively jostle. Multiple perspective swings us around the all-important drum in a rhythmic movement which is like the dance itself; the drum/sun becomes the hypnotic centre of a spiritual and cosmic system, the drummer reduced to insignificance compared with its power.

The purest expression of the iconic in Baker Lake graphics, however, is seen in the extraordinary series of formal hierarchical images by Jessie Oonark. In Oonark's scheme of things, the woman is predominant. In drawing after drawing, she is presented with such centrality and power as to suggest majesty rather than domesticity. "Heraldic" is a term sometimes applied to Oonark's designs, and a drawing like *Woman* (No. 9) explains why. The ulu, that universal tool of the Inuit woman, becomes her exclusive symbol in this drawing, as in many others by Oonark. It is her crest, supporter and motto, representing power and status. The ulu was essential in preparing food, so one might say that such drawings take the female role suggested by Kukiiyaut and elevate it from mere collaboration to almost priestly pre-eminence.

Although Oonark is perhaps best known for her portrayal of the woman in her art, she has in fact treated many other subjects. Her *Drum Dance* (No. 14) is a good example of the formalized, hieratic manner in which she celebrates traditional Inuit life. All her later drawings have a satisfying completeness, which is due not simply to their tight design, but, more subtly, to their paradoxical sense of closure. This closure that nevertheless implies repetition, because it is a closure derived from ritual, is by its nature always both continuous and fixed.

My aim in this essay is to suggest ways in which the Southern viewer might approach the Baker Lake drawings. There seems to be no way in which one can confidently tell just what the drawings mean to the artists themselves. The artists' comments, illuminating when dealing with facts about the drawings, tend otherwise to conceal more than they reveal. Take, for example,

Oonark's remarks about the ulus in her *Woman* (No. 9) discussed above: "A real human face doesn't really have the design of ulus," she says, "I just added those for decoration."[17] Possibly my comments on the function of the ulu say too much, but surely Oonark's say too little.

The interviews reveal little about the artist's emotions in an overt way, but, reading between the lines, it is difficult not to notice a strong sense of pleasure and discovery as the artists talk about their drawings. Most of the drawings deal with a traditional way of life that only the oldest of the artists would have experienced firsthand. For the others, that way of life exists only in the reports of elders - the legends and religious beliefs often now fragmentary and dreamlike.

Given the genesis of the art-making experiment at Baker Lake, the main purpose of which was to create a source of income by selling to a Southern market, there was a danger of spuriousness, that the Inuit artists would produce fake versions of 'Inuit life' for the South. The drawings themselves make it clear that this did not happen. It seems that in reaching back to the past, the artists made a profound discovery. They discovered themselves as a people. For this reason, it is not quite accurate to describe the drawings as nostalgic, nor to suggest that it is a "sad art."[18] They are not so much acts of remembrance as joyful records of self-recognition. To use a phrase applied by Elderfield in another context, these drawings are not "in the past tense."[19]

A significant feature of the drawings is the absence of any overt political content. There is no sense in them, for instance, of any conflict arising from the imposition of white power structures on a native system. Indeed there is no social critique at all, unless one interprets their somewhat idealized depiction of an earlier way of life as a gentle criticism of the present – an unconvincing proposition. As far as these drawings indicate, the Baker Lake artists are either not yet at the stage reached by many of their colleagues elsewhere, or are not of a similar frame of mind (some of them, of course, were old when they began drawing, and are now dead). There is nothing of "paradox, irony and ambivalence," the ingredients of individual awareness, and thence of political consciousness.[20] If the drawings are political at all, they are so in a rather remote sense, in that they are helping to establish a collective identity from which a political consciousness might eventually spring.

More or less instinctively, the Baker Lake artists developed a graphic mode that sprang naturally from their special way of looking at reality. But the North is changing socially, economically and politically, and with such change will come differences in artistic expression. One such development is already evident: Inuit artists are beginning to adopt more recognizably Southern modes of expression. Co-opting a Southern mode of representation, as William Noah does in his later drawings (No. 74, 75, 76, 77), is not as innocent as it may sound because, as suggested earlier, that mode implies an entire conceptual system.[21]

It might be advisable to abandon speculation about Inuit attitudes to their art and return to safer ground – the Southern response to the drawings. From the preceding discussion, it should now be clear what constitutes their appeal to an audience brought up in an entirely different cultural system. We are attracted by their freshness and liveliness, which strike anyone on the first glance. Then the exotic nature of their subjects both invites and teases us. On closer examination we are struck by the inventiveness and freedom of their technique, employing devices known to experimental 20th century art but not of it. Finally, though, it is the glimpse of a pristine simplicity, at least as perceived by us from outside, that gives them their greatest appeal. To illustrate this, we can turn once more to Elderfield and his discussion of, oddly enough, Jean Arp in his Dadaist period. According to Elderfield, Arp embraced a primitivism based on "the belief that what was wrong with modern civilization was its artificiality: that 'art' had corrupted 'nature'; that man's works had corrupted man's own nature and destroyed his original organic equilibrium." The Great War was a sign of such corruption and destruction, Elderfield goes on, and then he quotes Paul Fussell: "If the opposite of war is peace, the opposite of experiencing moments of war is proposing moments of pastoral." And that is what Arp proposed, says Elderfield: "a peaceable kingdom of the spontaneous and instinctive, populated by forms that escape contemporary suggestion to return through art what man's art had earlier destroyed."[22]

These words, which might be taken to describe a powerful movement in 20th century thought generally, could apply with extraordinary aptness to the Baker Lake drawings and indeed to Inuit art in general. One modification is needed, however: the Inuit pastoral, like all serious works in that genre, is not altogether peaceable. It shows a world where humans and nature are in balance, it is true, except that balance happens to be based on killing, and embraces fear. But absence of sentimentality makes the vision more powerful, and the fact remains that what the Baker Lake artists have produced, largely unconsciously and simply by remembering, is a pastoral for a South weary of war, of materialism and of urbanization.

Notes

1 Hal N. Opperman, "The Inuit Phenomenon in Art-historical Context," *Inuit Art Quarterly* 1:2 (Summer 1986): 1.

2 Daniel M. Mendelowitz. *Drawing* (New York: Holt, Reinhart and Winston, 1967): 35.

3 Peter A. Angeles, *Dictionary of Philosophy* (New York: Barnes and Noble, 1981): 279.

4 These endeavours are described by John Elderfield in his brilliant study, *The Modern Drawing: 100 Works on Paper from The Museum of Modern Art,* (New York: The Museum of Modern Art, 1983). My thinking about Inuit drawings owes much to the stimulating nature of this book.

5 For an account of the Butlers' work at Baker Lake, see: Sheila Butler, "The First Printmaking Year at Baker Lake," in *Inuit Art: An Anthology* (Winnipeg: Watson & Dwyer, 1988): 101-111. See also an untitled essay by Sheila Butler in *Baker Lake Prints and Print-Drawings 1970-76* (Winnipeg: Winnipeg Art Gallery, 1983): 13-17.

6 Jackson, Marion E. and William Noah trans., "Artists' Interpretations and Syllabic Translations for the Baker Lake Inuit Drawings in the Collection of the Macdonald Stewart Art Centre," photocopy manuscript (Guelph: Macdonald Stewart Art Centre, Spring 1983). Treatment of Inuit legends in relation to Inuit art is also found in: Bernadette Driscoll, *Inuit Myths, Legends and Songs* (Winnipeg: Winnipeg Art Gallery, 1982); C.H. Moore, *Keeveeok Awake! Mamnguqsualuk and the Rebirth of Legend at Baker Lake* (Edmonton: Ring House Gallery, University of Alberta, 1987). For a discussion of Baker Lake drawings which anticipates some of the points made in this essay, see untitled essay by Sheila Butler, in *Baker Lake Prints and Print-Drawings 1970-76,* (Winnipeg: Winnipeg Art Gallery, 1983): 13-17.

7 Jackson and Noah, 67.

8 Jackson and Noah, 55.

9 Jackson and Noah, 45.

10 Jackson and Noah, 19.

11 Jackson and Noah, 63.

12 Jackson and Noah, 62.

13 Jackson and Noah, 8.

14 Jackson and Noah, 34.

15 Medelowitz, 326.

16 Jackson and Noah, 19.

17 Jackson and Noah, 42.

18 Ronald Bloore, quoted by Jack Butler in: C.H. Moore, *Keeveeok Awake! Mamnguqsualuk and the Rebirth of Legend at Baker Lake* (Edmonton: Ring House Gallery, University of Alberta, 1986): 19.

19 John Elderfield, *The Modern Drawing: 100 Works on Paper from the Museum of Modern Art* (New York: Museum of Modern Art, 1983): 136.

20 This phrase is quoted from a review by Scott Watson of an exhibition entitled "Land, Spirit, Power: First Nations at the National Gallery of Canada," in *Canadian Art,* 10:1 (Spring 1993): 34-43. The review offers an intelligent analysis of the issues arising as native artists arrive at political consciousness in an alien culture.

21 Note, for instance, the nature of Noah's titles. *Sugarloaf Mountain* not only denotes a specific locale as opposed to the non-specific landscape in other drawings, but with the reference to the Jessie Oonark Arts and Crafts Centre, Noah links it with a recorded cultural history – one shared by both Inuit and white people. Similarly, his drawings *Drying Fish* and *Tea, Bannock and Biscuit,* are discrete, notational illustrations that might have been made by a white anthropologist or explorer: they seem to be looking at Inuit customs from without rather than from within. Noah here demonstrates a *consciousness* of drawing and its function that is absent from most of the other works in the exhibition and which, indeed, was largely absent from his own earlier drawings. They are 'knowing' drawings, or, as we would say in the South, Noah has achieved aesthetic distance.

22 Elderfield, 112.

Catalogue of the Exhibition

The 77 drawings in this exhibition were created by 19 of the major Baker Lake Inuit artists between 1959 and 1994. The drawings, all of which are in the collection of the Macdonald Stewart Art Centre, give a selective overview of the rich contemporary drawing tradition in Baker Lake.

Works in this catalogue are grouped by individual artist and are arranged in an approximate chronological order based on the birth date of the artist, thus allowing viewers to see developments through time. To aid viewers and researchers wishing supplementary information on the artists and the drawings, this catalogue includes summary biographies of the artists compiled by Sheila Ord using biographical materials provided by the Inuit Art Section of Indian and Northern Affairs Ottawa. Notes on individual drawings were prepared by Marion Jackson on the basis of interviews that Jackson and William Noah conducted with artists in Baker Lake in 1983 and 1985. These include additional information gained through further interviews with the artists conducted by William Noah, Marion Jackson, and Judith Nasby during October 1993. Additional statements were offered by artists during the Baker Lake Art Symposium in August 1994. To the extent possible, the artists' own words are used in interpreting the drawings; artists' comments are designated by italic typeface.

Individual artists are identified first by the most common spelling of their names. In cases where alternate spellings or alternate names exist, these are given in parentheses. All measurements refer to external dimensions of the drawing paper and are given in centimetres with height preceding width. Formal titles provided by the artists are indicated in italics; otherwise, descriptive titles are given in parentheses to aid in identification of works. Drawings marked with an ulu (⛏) indicate that they were part of the group of 43 works shown in Baker Lake from August 19 to 24, 1994 during the Baker Lake Art Symposium.

The term *Inuit* (singular *Inuk*) is used throughout this text to refer to the native people of the Canadian Arctic. These terms are preferred by the native people of the Canadian Arctic and, in their native Inuktitut language, mean "people" (singular "person").

Luke Anguhadluq (Anglosaglo; Angosaglo; Anguhalluq; Luq)

Born 1895 at Chantrey Inlet, died 1982. Moved to Baker Lake c.1961.

This lively drawing of an Inuk masterfully cracking his long whip to urge his dog team onward shows Anguhadluq's preference for experiences on the land as the subject matter in his art. The three dogs, their heads thrust energetically forward, each pull on an individual trace as is typical of the dog team harnessing system of the Central Arctic. This successful hunter returns to camp with many caribou on his sled.

Anguhadluq's signature is pencilled in Inuktitut syllabics above the head of the dog team driver and is oriented toward the top edge of the page. Anguhadluq was known to rotate the sheet as he worked, and he was not concerned with consistency of orientation.

When game became scarce, Luke Anguhadluq reluctantly abandoned traditional camp life and moved to Baker Lake where he continued to live in an iglu and tent until 1967. He was a prominent camp leader who was the father of Ruth Qualluaryuk and Mark Uqayuittaq (by adoption), the husband of Marion Tuu'luuq and cousin of Jessie Oonark, all of whom are represented in the exhibition. He began drawing in 1963 producing two to three drawings weekly. He also made some sculpture and participated in the Baker Lake print collections every year from 1972 until his death. Since 1972, Anguhadluq's work has appeared in over 70 exhibitions including *The Inuit Amautik: I Like My Hood to be Full*, Winnipeg Art Gallery, 1980; *L'estampe inuit*, National Museum of Man and Department of Indian and Northern Affairs, 1977-82; and *From the Centre: The Drawings of Luke Anguhadluq*, organized by the Art Gallery of Ontario, 1993-94. He is represented in numerous public collections including the Carleton University Art Gallery, Ottawa; The McMichael Canadian Art Collection, Kleinburg; the National Gallery of Canada, Ottawa and the Victoria and Albert Museum, London, England.

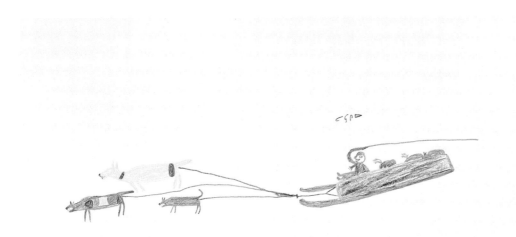

1   Luke Anguhadluq
     Untitled (dog team), 1969
     graphite and coloured pencil on paper
     48.3 x 60.9 cm
     Purchased with funds donated by Blount
     Canada Ltd., with assistance from the Ontario
     Government through the Ministry of Citizenship
     and Culture, 1980
     MS980.116

References:
     Jackson, Marion E. and Judith Nasby.
     Contemporary Inuit Drawings. Guelph, Ontario:
     Macdonald Stewart Art Centre, 1987, p.12.

Exhibitions:
*L'Art Inuit de la Collection Macdonald Stewart Art
     Centre*. Château Dufresne, Musée des Arts
     Décoratifs, Montreal, Quebec.
     December 9, 1982 - January 23, 1983.

Contemporary Inuit Drawings. Macdonald Stewart
     Art Centre, Guelph, Ontario. December 5, 1987
     - February 7, 1988 (toured in Canada and the
     United States in 1988-89) cat. no. 13.

*Contemporary Inuit Drawings from the Macdonald
     Stewart Art Centre Collection*. The
     Gallery/Stratford, Stratford, Ontario.
     September 6 - November 26, 1992.

In this drawing, Anguhadluq presents two adult figures and two children. The adults are presumably male as indicated by the straight lower hems of their parkas. Typical of Anguhadluq's style, the figures appear in visual isolation, perhaps simulating the visual experience of the Arctic itself where the diffuse white of the sky often blends seamlessly into the white of the snow and ice. It is not clear whether the artist intended to depict two men with children or whether he has portrayed the same man and child twice to indicate the movement of a man lifting a child to his shoulders. See No. 6, 42, 45-48, and 64 for examples of sequential actions within a single image.

Above the group of figures, Anguhadluq has pencilled an explanatory title, "Inuit" (meaning "the people").

2   Luke Anguhadluq

Inuit, 1969

graphite and coloured pencil on paper

60.7 x 48.2 cm

Purchased with funds donated by Blount
Canada Ltd., with assistance from
the Ontario Government through the Ministry
of Citizenship and Culture, 1980

MS980.121

A favoured theme in Anguhadluq's work, the drum dance was a communal activity with both social and religious significance in traditional Inuit culture. In this drawing, the spirited figure with the drum provides both a focus and energy for the figures rhythmically positioned around him. In a traditional drum dance, the drummer would swing the drum from side to side beating a hypnotic rhythm on the rim of the large circular drum. Jean Blodgett has noted that the drum was "not only a necessary accompaniment to the song contests and festive dances, it was also a significant component of the shamanic performance."*

William Noah has noted that Inuit in the area of Gjoa Haven used to have drum dances but that drum dances were generally discontinued in the Back River area after Canon James introduced Christian teachings. "We did not reject drum dancing. We just didn't do it" explained Noah, recalling his childhood in the Back River Area.**

* Jean Blodgett, *The Coming and Going of the Shaman* (Winnipeg: Winnipeg Art Gallery, 1979): 140.
** William Noah, in interview with Marion Jackson and Judith Nasby, October 1993.

3   Luke Anguhadluq
     Drum Dance, 1976
     graphite and coloured pencil on paper
     56.5 x 76.3 cm ⊥
     Purchased with funds donated by Blount
     Canada Ltd., with assistance from The
     Canada Council, 1982
     MS982.154

References:

Jackson, Marion E. and Judith Nasby. *Contemporary Inuit Drawings*. Guelph, Ontario: Macdonald Stewart Art Centre, 1987, p.94.

Exhibitions:

Inuit Art from the Permanent Collection. Macdonald Stewart Art Centre, Guelph, Ontario. June 5 - October 3, 1982.

L'Art Inuit de la Collection Macdonald Stewart Art Centre. Château Dufresne, Musée des Arts Décoratifs, Montreal, Quebec. December 9, 1982 - January 23, 1983.

Originale Inuit Tegninges fra Macdonald Stewart Art Centre, Canada. Musikhuset Aarhus, Denmark. April 25 - May 15, 1984 (toured in Denmark).

Contemporary Inuit Drawings. Macdonald Stewart Art Centre, Guelph, Ontario. December 5, 1987 - February 7, 1988 (toured in Canada and the United States in 1988-89), cat. no. 15.

Contemporary Inuit Drawings from the Macdonald Stewart Art Centre Collection. The Gallery/Stratford, Stratford, Ontario. September 6 - November 26, 1992.

For Inuit living inland away from the coast, as Anughadluq did during much of his adult life, fishing and hunting caribou were essential for survival. Therefore, it is not surprising that these themes are prominent in Anguhadluq's drawings. This particular drawing is unusual, however, as Anguhadluq presents a vertical row of male figures jigging for fish along the left edge of the page and fills the remaining two-thirds of the drawing with individuals catching, preparing and eating seal.

Anguhadluq most likely had the experience of seal hunting in the Chantrey Inlet area in his younger years. On rare occasions, seals from the Hudson Bay have come up the Chesterfield Inlet as far as Baker Lake. However, unlike Inuit living in coastal areas, Baker Lake Inuit traditionally depended for their survival almost exclusively on fish, caribou, muskox, and small ground animals rather than on seals and other sea mammals.

In her untitled drawing (cleaning fish) (No. 59), Ruth Annaqtuusi Tulurialik similarly combines activities relating to fishing with an image of a seal. Her explanatory comments about that drawing indicate how rarely seals come as far inland as Baker Lake.

4   Luke Anguhadluq
     Untitled (fishing), c.1976
     graphite and coloured pencil on paper
     66 x 101.6 cm ⊥
     Purchased with funds donated by Blount
     Canada Ltd., with assistance from The
     Canada Council, 1982
     MS982.165
References:
Jackson, Marion E. and Judith Nasby.
     Contemporary Inuit Drawings. Guelph,
     Ontario: Macdonald Stewart Art Centre, 1987,
     pp. 12, 13, 15, 25, 78.
Exhibitions:
Contemporary Inuit Drawings. Macdonald Stewart
     Art Centre, Guelph, Ontario. December 5, 1987
     - February 7, 1988 (toured in Canada and the
     United States in 1988-89), cat. no. 14.
*Contemporary Inuit Drawings from the Macdonald
     Stewart Art Centre Collection.*
     The Gallery/Stratford, Stratford, Ontario.
     September 6 - November 26, 1992.

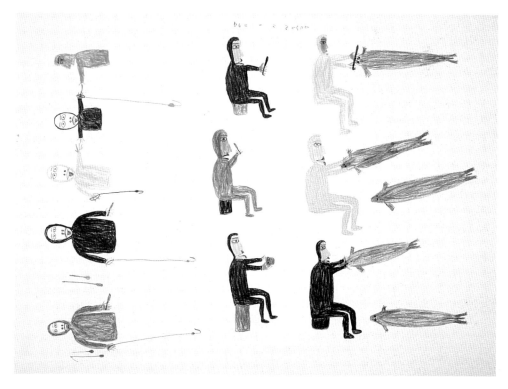

A considerable amount of cultural information is expressed in the drawings of early Baker Lake artists like Anguhadluq. This bold image portrays the distinct regional clothing style of the Western Arctic from the area around Coppermine or Cambridge Bay. The woman with her long narrow hood, full-shouldered parka and narrow *kiniq* (front apron) wears hair sticks in her stiff braids and exhibits the tattoo pattern typical of women in the Western Arctic in the 1920s and 1930s.

5 Luke Anguhadluq
   Untitled (figure with grey parka), 1977
   coloured pencil on paper
   75.5 x 56.5 cm
   Purchased with funds donated by Blount
   Canada Ltd., 1980
   MS980.053

Exhibitions:

*Inuit Drawings from the Macdonald Stewart Art
   Centre in Guelph.* Oakville Galleries/Gairloch,
   Oakville, Ontario. November 19, 1986 -
   January 4, 1987.

*Contemporary Inuit Drawings from the Macdonald
   Stewart Art Centre Collection.*
   The Gallery/Stratford, Stratford, Ontario.
   September 6 - November 26, 1992.

Jessie Oonark (Una; Unaaq)
Born 1906 in the Back River area, died 1985. Moved to Baker Lake in 1958.

Jessie Oonark was the mother of Janet Kigusiuq, Victoria Mamnguqsualuk, Nancy Pukingrnak and William Noah, and the cousin of Luke Anguhadluq, all of whom have drawings in the exhibition. Called "the Matriarch of Inuit Art" by art historian Bernadette Driscoll, this remarkable artist would sometimes produce 40 to 50 drawings in a week. She was one of the first artists to produce drawings for the Baker Lake print collections and was a leader among women artists who made wall hangings. Oonark illustrated *I Breathe A New Song*, an anthology of Inuit poetry edited by Richard Lewis in 1972. Her work has been included in over 100 Canadian and international exhibitions, 15 of them solo. They include *Oonark Wall Hangings*, National Arts Centre, 1971 and *Jessie Oonark: A Retrospective*, Winnipeg Art Gallery, 1986-88. Her work was part of *The Inuit Amautik: I Like My Hood to be Full*, Winnipeg Art Gallery, 1980 and *Northern Lights: Inuit Textile Art from the Canadian Arctic* organized by The Baltimore Museum of Art, 1993-94. Among the 36 public collections holding her work are the Art Gallery of Nova Scotia, Halifax; the Art Gallery of Ontario, Toronto; the Carleton University Art Gallery, Ottawa; the Art Gallery of Greater Victoria and the Winnipeg Art Gallery.

In this early graphite pencil drawing, Oonark filled the page with a series of events from Qiviuq's encounter with the unfriendly Naqaqongituk, a theme also explored by her daughter, Mamnguqsualuk (No. 48). Oonark explained the story:

That's the legend of Qiviuq and the two-headed dog and the unfriendly people. The backs of the legs of the unfriendly people are fleshless, and they cannot walk around. So, therefore, they had to ride on their two-headed dogs. This drawing is trying to tell the whole story. [Across the top of the drawing] Qiviuq is dressing, getting up. He is hiding there, and this is the leader giving advice to Qiviuq. This man is telling Qiviuq that he would have to aim right into the ear of the two-headed dog. If he misses, he would not survive. Every individual always has a leader giving advice. That's just one of the leaders giving advice to Qiviuq. Here [in the second row of images], Qiviuq is unfastening all the sleds during the night, planning to escape. While he was still hiding, the sons of this man by the iglu came in, and the family is inside the iglu. These two sons were some of the best hunters. They just came back, and they smelled the scent of Qiviuq. They started asking if somebody is hiding and said that he should show himself. It shows very little here because of the size of the iglu. [In the lower right corner], Qiviuq is escaping and is aiming at the dog as he was told to do. Qiviuq was told to aim at the lump that is part of the ear, that part exactly. That's exactly what he's doing. If he missed the ear part of the dog, he would be attacked by the two-headed dog. It was really a scary story!*

*Jessie Oonark, in interview with Marion Jackson and William Noah, Spring 1983.

6   Jessie Oonark
    Qiviuq and the Two-Headed Dog, 1959-1963
    graphite on paper
    60.7 x 48.1 cm ⚖
    Purchased with funds donated by Blount
    Canada Ltd., with assistance from
    the Ontario Government through the Ministry
    of Citizenship and Culture, 1980
    MS980.095
Exhibitions:
*Originale Inuit Tegninges fra Macdonald Stewart Art
    Centre, Canada*. Musikhuset Aarhus,Denmark.
    April 25 - May 15, 1984 (toured in Denmark).
Jessie Oonark: A Retrospective. Winnipeg Art Gallery.
    November 16, 1986 - February15,1987, no. 8.
    p.30.

Respected for her boldly patterned wall hangings and for her graphic works, Jessie Oonark had an extraordinary sense of design. She frequently incorporated the abstract shape of the *ulu*, a traditional woman's knife, to express her own sense of womanhood and to create a visual pattern in her works. This drawing, which literally and figuratively positions woman at the centre, epitomizes Oonark's interest in the theme of womanhood. Explaining the drawing, she said:

Those are tattoos on the woman's face. I remember when some of the women would have tattoos on their arms as well as on their chests. They looked very pretty.

I didn't want to have tattoos myself. They said they wanted to put tattoos on my arms and my face, but I didn't want them to do it. Then, if you didn't want to have tattoos, they would just leave you alone. The tattoos were just for attractiveness. That's the way they used to do it in the olden days. But, if a person didn't want to have tattoos, the person didn't need to have tattoos.

A real human face doesn't really have the design of ulus. I just added those for decoration.*

*Jessie Oonark, in interview with Marion Jackson and William Noah, Spring 1983.

9   Jessie Oonark
Woman, c.1972
graphite and coloured pencil on paper
28 x 33 cm
Purchased with funds donated by Blount
Canada Ltd., with assistance from the Ontario
Government through the Ministry of Citizenship
and Culture, 1980
MS980.129

Exhibitions:

L'Art Inuit de la Collection Macdonald Stewart Art Centre. Château Dufresne, Musée des Arts Décoratifs, Montreal, Quebec. December 9, 1982 - January 23, 1983.

Originale Inuit Tegninges fra Macdonald Stewart Art Centre, Canada. Musikhuset Aarhus, Denmark. April 25 - May 15, 1984 (toured in Denmark).

Inuit Drawings from the Macdonald Stewart Art Centre in Guelph. Oakville Galleries/Gairloch, Oakville, Ontario. November 19, 1986 - January 4, 1987.

Inuit Art from the Collection. Macdonald Stewart Art Centre, Guelph, Ontario.
January 4 - August 1, 1993.

Discussing the autobiographical nature of this drawing, Oonark said:

The top image is a raft we used for crossing a river or a lake. And the bottom image is the first time I ever saw a canoe, that day we got the first family allowance. That's myself and my children. It wasn't exactly like that, but that's an interpretation of what the canoe looked like. These are white man's clothing with stripes.

As for the stripes on the raft, we would use caribou skins, one fur-side up and one fur-side down, side-by-side. Some younger people riding on the raft would be lying down and staying very still. This is just a raft, and the adult is taking those others across. I have myself ridden like this a lot of times. I was afraid at first, but it is safer than a kayak, much wider. The person on the back of the raft is supposed to be afraid to go across.

The first time our family allowance was received, we had a lot of cash and we bought a canoe and a sewing machine at the same time! It was the very first canoe that I ever had, and I even asked my brother-in-law to go and get it. It was a really nice canoe. It came from Baker Lake. That is me (on the end) and those are my kids and my husband in the canoe.*

*Jessie Oonark, in interview with Marion Jackson and William Noah, Spring 1983.

10 Jessie Oonark
    Family Crossing by Raft and Kayak, 1974
    coloured pencil on paper
    56 x 75.5 cm
    Purchased with funds donated by Blount
    Canada Ltd., 1980
    MS980.033
Exhibitions:
*L'Art Inuit de la Collection Macdonald Stewart Art
    Centre.* Château Dufresne, Musée des Arts
    Décoratifs, Montreal, Quebec. December 9,
    1982 - January 23, 1983.
*Contemporary Inuit Drawings from the Macdonald
    Stewart Art Centre Collection.*
    The Gallery/Stratford, Stratford, Ontario.
    September 6 - November 26, 1992.

Jessie Oonark's comments about this drawing are extremely helpful in understanding both its content and its formal qualities:

Those are two women chanting and singing, and the men with the birds on their heads are shamans. They're just standing there, listening. They're just there to listen.

*The thing up there between the two women is just there to decorate it. Sometimes when there is an open space, I just draw up something else, add it onto the drawing.**

*Jessie Oonark, in interview with Marion Jackson and William Noah, Spring 1983.

11   Jessie Oonark
      Faces, 1978
      graphite and coloured pencil on paper
      48.8 x 70.2 cm
      Purchased with funds donated by Blount
      Canada Ltd., with assistance from
      the Ontario Government through the Ministry
      of Citizenship and Culture, 1980
      MS980.135
Exhibitions:
*Inuit Drawings from the Macdonald Stewart Art
      Centre in Guelph.* Oakville Galleries/Gairloch,
      Oakville, Ontario. November 19, 1986 -
      January 4, 1987.

Jessie Oonark was particularly known for her excellent sewing skills. As a young girl, she had learned to clean and cut skins to make the tailored caribou skin garments in the style of the people from the Back River area. Her skills in sewing as well as the perceptual skills she developed in making patterns and judging proportion facilitated her later work, especially wall hangings and drawing. This drawing, compelling in its own right, gives valuable information about the shapes and proportions of patterns pieces for traditional clothing.

Those are patterns that are ready to be sewn together for clothing, caribou skins for clothing. This is going to be an amautiq (woman's parka) *and a hood and the socks. It's not put together yet.* *

*Jessie Oonark, in interview with Marion Jackson and William Noah, Spring 1983.

12   Jessie Oonark
     Cutout Pieces for an Amautiq, Hood and Socks
     (schematic clothing patterns), 1978
     coloured pencil on paper
     38.1 x 56.4 cm
     Purchased with funds donated by Blount
     Canada Ltd., 1980
     MS980.034
Exhibitions:
*Contemporary Inuit Drawings from the Macdonald
     Stewart Art Centre Collection.*
     The Gallery/Stratford, Stratford, Ontario.
     September 6 - November 26, 1992.

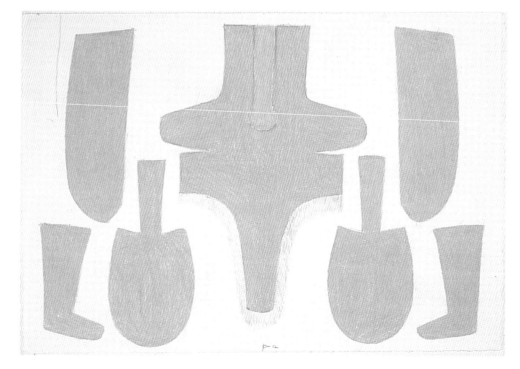

Oonark's remarks about this drawing reveal her keen power of observation and her interest in regional variations in clothing design. William Noah noted that Tookoome and his family who came from Gjoa Haven were wearing this type of clothing the first time he saw them.

I saw Iluiliaqmiut people when I was very small, the way they dress and the way they look. The were really excellent dancers. One person, while beating the drum, could be singing at the same time. That's not like any other people!

When I had my first child, I saw them again. They lived straight out across Chantrey Inlet in the coastal area. It was those people I was thinking about when I made this drawing.

At first, those people had a very high cut of parka, but later, probably influenced by the western arctic people, they stopped wearing those. The clothing in this drawing is a sort of second fashion. As time went by, somebody must have changed their style of clothing. Earlier they had a very high cut of parka with a very narrow tail in back, and the fronts were really thin too. *

*Jessie Oonark, in interview with Marion Jackson and William Noah, Spring 1983.

13   Jessie Oonark
     Iluiliaqmiut People, 1978
     graphite and coloured pencil on paper
     76.2 x 56.2 cm
     Purchased with funds donated by Blount
     Canada Ltd., 1980
     MS980.044

Exhibitions:

L'Art Inuit de la Collection Macdonald Stewart Art Centre. Château Dufresne, Musée des Arts Décoratifs, Montreal, Quebec. December 9, 1982 - January 23, 1983.

Originale Inuit Tegninges fra Macdonald Stewart Art Centre, Canada. Musikhuset Aarhus, Denmark. April 25 - May 15, 1984 (toured in Denmark).

Inuit Art from the Collection. Macdonald Stewart Art Centre, Guelph, Ontario.
January 4 - August 1, 1993.

Her mind filled with memories of the more than 50 years that she lived the traditional camp life in the Back River area, Oonark frequently made drawings reflecting these experiences. For her and for her cousin, Luke Anguhadluq, the drum dance was a favoured theme (No. 3). Both of these artists shared memories of the times of *qaqqiq* (gathering) when people from different camps would come together, particularly during winter to feast and enjoy drum dancing and singing in a large common iglu. Oonark said of this drawing:

This is a really big snow house, and there's a dance. The people on the floor are the drum dancers, and the people in the back are the people who are singing.

This could be a stone house or even a stone shelter for trapping birds - except it doesn't have an entrance! Those people are singing in the back. They're people singing for the drum dancer.

I myself don't know any Inuit songs. I don't do any drum dancing or singing at all. *

It is interesting to compare this drawing to the previous drawing (No. 13) and to note that the dancers in the front of the iglu wear clothing similar to that of the excellent dancers Oonark remembered from her youth as Iluiliaqmiut from the coastal area beyond Chantrey Inlet.

*Jessie Oonark, in interview with Marion Jackson and William Noah, Spring 1983.

14　Jessie Oonark

Drum Dance, 1978

graphite and coloured pencil on paper

56.7 x 75.9 cm ⚓

Purchased with funds donated by Blount Canada Ltd., 1980

MS980.132

References:

Nasby, Judith. "Collections: Macdonald Stewart Art Centre," *Inuit Arts and Crafts* 2 (1984):38.

Blodgett, Jean and Marie Bouchard. *Jessie Oonark: A Retrospective*. Winnipeg: Winnipeg Art Gallery, 1986, illustrated p.50.

Jackson, Marion E. and Judith Nasby. *Contemporary Inuit Drawings*. Guelph, Ontario: Macdonald Stewart Art Centre, 1987, pp.23, 27.

Exhibitions:

Inuit Art from the Permanent Collection. Macdonald Stewart Art Centre, Guelph, Ontario. June 5 - October 3, 1982.

L'Art Inuit de la Collection Macdonald Stewart Art Centre. Château Dufresne, Musée des Arts Décoratifs, Montreal, Quebec. December 9, 1982 - January 23, 1983.

Contemporary Inuit Drawings. Macdonald Stewart Art Centre, Guelph, Ontario. December 5, 1987 - February 7, 1988 (toured in Canada and the United States in 1988-89), cat. no. 62.

Contemporary Inuit Drawings from the Macdonald Stewart Art Centre Collection. The Gallery/Stratford, Stratford, Ontario. September 6 - November 26, 1992.

Inuit Art from the Collection. Macdonald Stewart Art Centre, Guelph, Ontario. September 20, 1993 - September 15, 1994.

Never merely an illustrator, Oonark re-works traditional themes often bringing together seemingly unrelated images which, in their combination, convey extraordinary insight into the complex cultural heritage of the Inuit. Of these heraldic women/fish figures, Oonark said simply:

Those two ladies are chanting and singing. They have a kind of a fish body. It's only a piece of paper, and I just added those fish images onto those ladies there. I just drew this from my mind.

It is interesting to compare this drawing with *Faces*, another of Oonark's images of throat-singing (No. 11). In both drawings, Oonark seems to have conflated the subject of throat-singing and shamanism. In this drawing, she combines throat singing with half-woman/half-fish sea creatures, perhaps suggestive of Talalayu, the powerful spirit who lives under the sea and controls the sea mammals.

*Jessie Oonark, in interview with Marion Jackson and William Noah, Spring 1983.

15   Jessie Oonark
      Untitled (fish women), 1975
      graphite and coloured pencil on paper
      56.4 x 76 cm
      Purchased with funds donated by Blount Ltd.,
      with assistance from the Ontario
      Government through the Ministry of Citizenship
      and Culture, 1980
      MS980.134

References:

Jackson, Marion E. and Judith Nasby. *Contemporary Inuit Drawings*. Guelph, Ontario: Macdonald Stewart Art Centre, 1987, pp.23, 26.

Nasby, Judith. *Contemporary Inuit Drawings/Dessins inuit contemporains*. Guelph, Ontario: Macdonald Stewart Art Centre, 1989 (exhibition catalogue, abridged version) no. 5, p.9.

Exhibitions:

Inuit Art from the Permanent Collection. Macdonald Stewart Art Centre, Guelph, Ontario. June 5 - October 3, 1982.

L'Art Inuit de la Collection Macdonald Stewart Art Centre. Château Dufresne, Musée des Arts Décoratifs, Montreal, Quebec. December 9, 1982 - January 23, 1983.

Contemporary Inuit Drawings. Macdonald Stewart Art Centre, Guelph, Ontario. December 5, 1987 - February 7, 1988 (toured in Canada and the United States in 1988-89), cat. no. 61.

Contemporary Inuit Drawings from the Macdonald Stewart Art Centre Collection. The Gallery/Stratford, Stratford, Ontario. September 6 - November 26, 1992.

Marion Tuu'luuq (Anguhadluq; Tudluq; Tuu'luq; Tulluq; Toodlook)

Born in 1910 at Chantrey Inlet. Moved to Baker Lake c.1961.

Marion Tuu'luuq is the widow of Luke Anguhadluq. In the 1960s Tuu'luuq worked on wall hangings and about 1970 she began drawing. By 1974 her prints were included in the annual print collection. This was the same year that one of her wall hangings was chosen for the World Crafts Council exhibition *In Praise of Hands*. Since then Tuu'luuq's work has been featured in nearly 50 exhibitions including *Contemporary Indian and Inuit Art of Canada*, (Department of Indian Affairs and Northern Development), presented at the General Assembly Building, United Nations, 1983-85; *Baker Lake Prints & Print-Drawings: 1970-1976*, Winnipeg Art Gallery, 1983; *Marion Tuu'luq Wallhangings*, The Upstairs Gallery, Winnipeg, 1980 and *Northern Lights: Inuit Textiles from the Canadian Arctic*, The Baltimore Museum of Art, 1993-94. Her art has become part of the permanent collections of the Simon Fraser Gallery, Burnaby; the Carleton University Art Gallery, Ottawa; the National Gallery of Canada, Ottawa and the Art Gallery of Ontario, Toronto. In 1990, Tuu'luuq received an honorary Doctor of Laws Degree from the University of Alberta, Edmonton.

Drawings by Baker Lake artists give access to the rich oral tradition of the central Canadian Arctic. Just as storytellers might embellish stories giving them an individual interpretation, so do the artists making the drawings. This is illustrated by comparing this drawing with Jessie Oonark's drawing of *Two Stories* (No. 8) which includes the same story that Tuu'luuq relates:

*This is the legend of Kukiiyuaq, a man with very long fingernails. I can't really tell the story of Kukiiyuaq in detail. I can't really remember everything about it, but I heard about it. The story is that there was a man and his sister walking. They came to a camp where the Kukiiyuaq people were living. The man and his sister were really thirsty from walking a long time. The man asked his sister to go into the iglu and ask for some water. When the sister peeked through the doorway and asked for water, these Kukiiyuaqs asked her to take off her parka because the snow house was dripping. She did as she was told and took off her parka. Then she grabbed a bucket of water and started to walk out the door, but these Kukiiyuaqs started scratching her back with their long fingernails. Her brother had told her to yell if she needed help, and she screamed for help. And her brother saved her just in time from being torn apart. It's a scary story. The drawing is a mixture of the story about the Kukiiyuaq and an animal drawing. Just from my mind, I drew that the Kukiiyuaq is trying to grab a caribou. Those two images at the top are just fish. I sort of decorated them. They have nothing to do with the story.**

*Marion Tuu'luuq, in interview with Marion Jackson and William Noah, Spring 1983.

16 Marion Tuu'luuq

Untitled (story of Kukiiyuaq), 1974
graphite and coloured pencil on paper
56 x 76 cm ⬲
Purchased with funds donated by Blount
Canada Ltd., with assistance from
the Ontario Government through the Ministry
of Citizenship and Culture, 1980
MS980.150

Reference:
Nasby, Judith. "Collections: Macdonald Stewart Art
     Centre," *Inuit Arts and Crafts* 2 (1984):37.

Exhibitions:
Contemporary Inuit Drawings. Macdonald Stewart
     Art Centre, Guelph, Ontario. December 5, 1987
     - February 7, 1988 (toured in Canada and the
     United States in 1988-89), cat. no. 29.

Tuu'luuq's facile imagination is evident in this drawing in which she surrounds a central bird image with a fish and land animals. The bird, with its outstretched wings and extended talons, seems to be hunting the fish and animals below. The animals in the lower corners of the drawing, however, are given wings so that they too may take flight. Such transformations are common in Tuu'luuq's optimistic work where identity has a fluidity which provides animals and humans uncanny abilities for escaping danger and maintaining well-being.

17   Marion Tuu'luuq
Untitled (bird, fish and transforming animals),
1975
coloured pencil on paper
56 x 76 cm
Purchased with funds donated by Blount
Canada Ltd., 1993
MS993.029

Tuu'luuq's drawings and wall hangings give access to her thoughts and to her memories. This enigmatic drawing has been explained by Marion Tuu'luuq as follows:

This is a polar bear. As children, we used to look through snow and pretend to see bears, so this is a polar bear. These (radiating forms) *are places where the polar bear would hide.**

* Marion Tuu'luuq, Baker Lake Art Symposium, August 1994.

18 Marion Tuu'luuq
    Untitled (watching a polar bear),
    coloured pencil on paper
    56 x 76 cm ⏇
    Purchased with funds donated by Blount
    Canada Ltd., 1993
    MS993.051

Both Tuu'luuq and Irene Avaalaaqiaq (No. 64) have made drawings that they relate to a partially remembered story about a fish that swallows humans. In both Tuu'luuq's and Avaalaaqiaq's recollections of this story, a bird is also present. Avaalaaqiaq suggests that the human transforms into a bird after being swallowed by the fish, whereas Tuu'luuq's presentation of the bird is more ambiguous. Upon seeing this drawing a number of years after she made it, Tuu'luuq said:

I am happy with this drawing. This is a drawing of a bird. The faces are in the bird, and it has the head of a bird. I have heard of a legend about a fish that had a human head and also ate two human beings. That is what I drew out of a legend that I have heard. The caribou is looking at the bird and the fish.*

* Marion Tuu'luuq, Baker Lake Art Symposium, August 1994.

19   Marion Tuu'luuq
     Untitled (fish that swallows humans)
     coloured pencil on paper
     56 x 76 cm ⟁
     Purchased with funds donated by Blount
     Canada Ltd., 1993
     MS993.052

Martha Ittuluka'naaq (Etoolookutna; Ittulukatnak; Itoolookutna; Ittoolookutna)

Born 1912 in the Kazan River area, died 1981. Moved to Baker Lake c.1960.

Martha Ittuluka'naaq began drawing in the 1960s. Her drawings and prints have been shown in approximately 20 exhibitions, such as *The Inuit Print/L'estampe inuit*, organized by the Canadian Museum of Man and the Department of Indian Affairs and Northern Development, 1977-82; *Baker Lake Prints & Print-Drawings 1970-76*, Winnipeg Art Gallery, 1983; *Espaces Inuit*, Maison Hamel-Bruneau, Ste-Foy, Quebec, 1991 and *The Gift Collection of Frederick and Lucy S. Herman*, Joseph and Margaret Muscarelle Museum of Art, Williamsburg, Virginia, 1993. The Canadian Museum of Civilization, Hull; the Inuit Cultural Institute, Rankin Inlet and the Anchorage Museum of History and Art, Alaska are some of the public collections which hold her work.

Reminiscent of 19th-century incised ivory hunting tallies from the Western Arctic, this small drawing portrays ordered rows of caribou in profile. It is executed in an extremely abbreviated style characteristic of Martha Ittuluka'naaq's work. With uncommon directness and economy of design, Ittuluka'naaq uses only two lines to construct each animal; a single uninterrupted line to establish the front leg, head, back, and hind leg, and a second line to establish the other front leg, underbelly, and rear leg of each caribou. Ittuluka'naaq's re-drawing of these contour lines may reflect her hesitancy in drawing images on paper, an activity for which she had no training and virtually no prior experience. The resultant gestural quality of line imparts a lively energy to the drawing.

20 Martha Ittuluka'naaq
Animals, 1969-1970
graphite on paper
14 x 10.5 cm ⊼
Purchased with funds donated by Blount Canada Ltd., with assistance from the Ontario Government through the Ministry of Citizenship and Culture, 1980
MS980.124

References:

Nasby, Judith. "Collections: Macdonald Stewart Art Centre," *Inuit Arts and Crafts* 2 (1984):41.

Jackson, Marion E. and Judith Nasby. *Contemporary Inuit Drawings*. Guelph, Ontario: Macdonald Stewart Art Centre, 1987, pp.12, 25, 69, 70.

Exhibitions:

Contemporary Inuit Drawings. Macdonald Stewart Art Centre, Guelph, Ontario. December 5, 1987 - February 7, 1988 (toured in Canada and the United States in 1988-89), cat. no. 7a.

Contemporary Inuit Drawings from the Macdonald Stewart Art Centre Collection. The Gallery/Stratford, Stratford, Ontario. September 6 - November 26, 1992.

Inuit Art from the Collection. Macdonald Stewart Art Centre, Guelph, Ontario. January 4 - August 1, 1993.

When the Inuit of Baker Lake were first given paper and encouraged to make drawings, many filled the drawing papers with a generous number of separate figures in varying orientations on the page. This drawing by Martha Ittuluka'naaq is of that type. The individual human figures, the land animals (one of which is nursing a cub), and the kneeling woman jigging for fish seem to have little or no relationship to one another. The fact that a disproportionately large fish overlaps and almost obliterates a small male figure seems to have been unproblematic for the artist. The fish and human seem to co-exist rather easily in the same space.

It appears that Ittuluka'naaq focused her attention on each individual figure or animal as she drew it, creating as a by-product an overall structure in which the 'whole' has evolved from the interaction of separate 'parts.' This approach differs markedly from the hierarchical structuring characteristic of most Western art from the Renaissance to the present day.

21   Martha Ittuluka'naaq
     Untitled (seven humans, six land animals and a
     fish), 1970
     graphite and coloured pencil on paper
     75.9 x 55.9 cm
     Purchased with funds donated by Blount
     Canada Ltd., with assistance from
     the Ontario Government through the Ministry of
     Citizenship and Culture, 1980
     MS980.052

As a woman who grew to maturity on the land in the traditional Inuit culture, Martha Ittuluka'naaq developed skills for preparing skins, sewing, and for judging size and proportion for the construction of fur garments. Her interest in clothing and her awareness of regional clothing patterns provided her with a rich source of imagery when she began to draw. The male and female clothing styles detailed in the lower left quadrant of this drawing are typical Keewatin area styles.

22   Martha Ittuluka'naaq
      Untitled (group of animals and figures with kayak), 1970
      coloured pencil on paper
      55.7 x 38.3 cm ⌖
      Purchased with funds donated by Blount Canada Ltd., 1980
      MS980.069

Françoise Oklaga (Katalik; Qattalik; Oklooga)

Born 1924 in Coral Harbour, died 1991. Moved to Baker Lake in 1975 after living in Chesterfield Inlet.

Oklaga was in her early 50s when she first began to draw, and her lively, gestural style remained constant through the fifteen years that she made images on paper. Characteristically, she filled the entire drawing page with colourful human figures and animals in inventive juxtapositions, filling the background with colour that imparted a raw energy and directness to her drawings.

A hallmark of Oklaga's art is her frequent use of wide, starring eyes, usually drawn as if seen from the front even when figures are depicted in profile. This device gives her drawings an 'archaic' quality similar to the stylization in Egyptian art.

In this drawing two human figures emerge from a snow iglu while two other human figures, a bird, and a small ground animal (a fox?) seem to float in the space above the iglu. Oklaga's images are whimsical, drawn freely and not restricted by conventions of logic or naturalistic perspective.

Françoise Oklaga was the sister of Cape Dorset artist, Pudlo Pudlat, though she was adopted as an infant to a family in Chesterfield Inlet. She began drawing in 1976 and also made prints and wall hangings. A solo exhibition *Coloured Drawings by Francoise Oklaga of Baker Lake* was held in 1982 at the Isaacs/Innuit Gallery, Toronto. Other exhibitions that include her work are *Contemporary Inuit Drawings: The Gift Collection of Frederick and Lucy S. Herman*, Joseph and Mary Muscarelle Museum of Art, Williamsburg, Virginia, 1993-94 and *Patiently I Sing, Selections from the Tyler/Brooks Collection*, Carleton University Art Gallery, 1994. Oklaga is represented in The Canada Council Art Bank, Ottawa; the Prince of Wales Northern Heritage Centre, Yellowknife and the Winnipeg Art Gallery.

23   Françoise Oklaga
Iglu and Figures
coloured pencil on paper
56 x 38 cm
Purchased with funds donated by Blount
Canada Ltd., 1993
MS993.026

Because Françoise Oklaga spoke very little about the specific meaning she intended in her drawings, interpretations are speculative. This drawing seems to represent a solitary man safely enclosed in an iglu with his thoughts of animals (perhaps wolves) dressed in human clothing. The animals, wearing beautifully tailored traditional garments of the Keewatin, reach toward one another, interacting as humans attracted to one another. The wavy lines and dashes outside the iglu may suggest a howling winter storm. In a drawing on what may be a related theme, Irene Avaalaaqiaq presents a person on the land with images in his mind (No. 66).

The oral traditions of the Arctic abound with stories of animals pursuing activities parallel to those of human beings. These animal stories not only provided entertainment for youngsters in the old days (often embodied in a moralizing context similar to Aesop's fables), they also incorporated information about behavioral patterns of animal species useful in a hunting culture. A memory of such stories and the experience of having imaginary visions when alone on the land may have inspired Oklaga's drawing.

24 Françoise Oklaga
    Untitled (Inuk with animals in human clothing)
    coloured pencil on paper
    56 x 76 cm
    Purchased with funds donated by Blount
    Canada Ltd., 1993
    MS993.044

This enigmatic image of human and wolf heads alternating in a tight circle may be a representation of a human being's thoughts. In this case, the thoughts may be of a wolf or wolves with the thinker becoming progressively more frightened as the thought continues to revolve in his mind. Perhaps Oklaga, like Irene Avaalaaqiaq, uses a progression of colour in the human faces to register the person's rising terror as the mental images of the wolves become increasingly real and threatening (No. 67). As in Avaalaaqiaq's drawing, the background coloration in Oklaga's drawing may suggest the tundra, positioning the thinking person alone on the land.

25 Françoise Oklaga
    Untitled (human heads and wolf heads)
    coloured pencil on paper
    56 x 76 cm
    Purchased with funds donated by Blount
    Canada Ltd., 1993
    MS993.045

In this drawing, the central head in profile appears to be that of a person talking, most likely to the two people in front and perhaps about the animals emerging from the front and rear of the speaker's head and throat. The animal heads seem to flow from the speaker as articulated thoughts, animating both the speaker and the pictorial space.

Oklaga's love of texture is evident not just in her gestural manner of applying heavy wax pencil but in her habit of making her drawings on top of corrugated cardboard surfaces to enliven the drawing through the added texture of the corrugation.

26   Françoise Oklaga
     Untitled (humans and animals)
     56 x 76 cm
     coloured pencil on paper
     Purchased with funds donated by Blount
     Canada Ltd., 1993
     MS993.046

Mark Uqayuittuq (Oqaiyituk; Oyayeetok; Uqayuittaq; Uqayuittuk)
Born 1925 in Back River area, died 1984. Moved to Baker Lake in the early 1960s.

A very interesting though not prolific draftsman, Mark Uqayuittuq produced a relatively small body of work dealing with themes from traditional legends and experience on the land. This drawing seems to relate to the story of the human- headed fish that swallows human beings. This same story inspired drawings by Marion Tuu'luuq (No. 19) and Irene Avaalaaqiaq (No. 64).

Uqayuittuq was the adopted son of Luke Anguhadluq and the husband of Janet Kigusiuq, both of whom are represented in this exhibition. His media included drawings, sculpture and prints. Uqayuittuq began exhibiting in 1972 in *Eskimo Fantastic Art*, Gallery III, School of Art, University of Manitoba. He was also featured in a solo exhibition *Mark Uqayuittaq - Sculpture and Drawing*, Image of the Inuit, Los Angeles in 1980. Among other group exhibitions were *Prints & Print-Drawings 1970-76*, Winnipeg Art Gallery, 1983 and *Inuit Graphics and Drawings from 1959-1990*, Arctic Artistry, Hastings-on-Hudson, New York, 1990. He is represented in the collections of the Art Gallery of Greater Victoria; the Carleton University Art Gallery, Ottawa; the Canadian Guild of Crafts, Montreal; The Canada Council Art Bank, Ottawa and the Winnipeg Art Gallery.

27 Mark Uqayuittuq
Untitled (fish that swallows humans)
graphite and coloured pencil on paper
50.9 x 65.8 cm
Purchased with funds donated by Blount
Canada Ltd., with assistance from
the Ontario Government through the Ministry of
Citizenship and Culture, 1980
MS980.156
Exhibitions:
Contemporary Inuit Drawings from the Macdonald Stewart Art Centre Collection.
The Gallery/Stratford, Stratford, Ontario.
September 6 - November 26, 1992.

This complex drawing appears to combine an image of a shaman in flight (upper left corner) with a vision of animals and an episode from the traditional legend about the dog/children who became the ancestors of the white race. Uqayuittuq's sister-in-law, Victoria Mamnguqsualuk, made a number of drawings based on this same legend and her account of the story is helpful in understanding this image (No. 44).

In Uqayuittuq's drawing, the standing figure in the centre appears to be the legendary selfish grandfather who dictated that his daughter marry a dog. In this particular episode of the story, the grandfather is greeted by two of his dog/human grandchildren who lick the grandfather's face in feigned good will. The unsuspecting grandfather does not realize that this greeting is prefatory to the grandchildren pouncing on him and killing him in retaliation for his mistreatment of his daughter and grandchildren.

28 Mark Uqayuittuq
Untitled (greeting of the dog/children)
graphite and coloured pencil on paper
50.8 x 66 cm
Purchased with funds donated by Blount Canada Ltd., with assistance from the Ontario Government through the Ministry of Citizenship and Culture, 1980
MS980.157

Janet Kigusiuq (Keegooseot; Keegoaseat; Keegooseeot)
Born 1926 in the Back River/Garry Lake area. Moved to Baker Lake in the early 1960s.

In this drawing, Janet Kigusiuq depicts the traditional Inuit legend about the creation of the sun and the moon. While there are regional variations in this legend, most versions feature a young woman who is visited nightly by a young man with whom she has intimate relations. Eager to ascertain the identity of the young man, the young woman marks the young man's face one night with soot from her stone lamp in order to identify him when she sees him in the dance house. Later at the dance house, she discovers that the young man is her brother. In embarrassment and anguish, she flees from the dance house carrying a torch and is followed by her brother whose torch goes out as he pursues her. Together they rise into the sky where she becomes the sun and he becomes the moon.*

* See: Knud Rasmussen, *Intellectual Culture of the Iglulik Eskimos*. Report of the Fifth Thule Expedition 1921-24, vol. 7, no. 1. (Copenhagen: Gyldendal, 1929), pp. 77-81.

Janet Kigusiuq is the eldest daughter of Jessie Oonark, sister of Victoria Mamnguqsualuk, Nancy Pukingrnak and William Noah and widow of Mark Uqayuittuq, all of whom are represented in this exhibition. Her primary media are drawings and appliqué felt and wool duffle wall hangings which she has made since the 1970s. A solo exhibition held in 1993 at Galerie Brousseau & Brousseau in Quebec, featured her drawings. Kigusiuq's work has been included in over 80 Canadian and international exhibitions including *The People Within - Art from Baker Lake*, Art Gallery of Ontario, 1976; *Inuit Myths, Legends and Songs*, Winnipeg Art Gallery, 1982-83; *Die Kunst aus der Arktis*, (Indian and Northern Affairs Canada) presented by Commerzbank Frankfurt, Germany, 1985-86 and *Northern Lights: Inuit Art from the Canadian Arctic*, The Baltimore Museum of Art, 1993-94. Institutions which hold her work include the Agnes Etherington Art Centre, Kingston; the Carleton University Art Gallery, Ottawa; the National Gallery of Canada, Ottawa; the Art Gallery of Ontario, Toronto and the Winnipeg Art Gallery.

29   Janet Kigusiuq
Sun and Moon
graphite and coloured pencil on paper
56.5 x 76.5 cm
Purchased with funds donated by Blount
Canada Ltd., with assistance from
The Canada Council, 1982
MS982.173
Exhibitions:
L'Art Inuit de la Collection Macdonald Stewart Art Centre. Château Dufresne, Musée des Arts Décoratifs, Montreal, Quebec. December 9, 1982 - January 23, 1983.

Inuit Drawings from the Macdonald Stewart Art Centre in Guelph. Oakville Galleries/Gairloch, Oakville, Ontario. November 19, 1986 - January 4, 1987.

Contemporary Inuit Drawings from the Macdonald Stewart Art Centre Collection. The Gallery/Stratford, Stratford, Ontario. September 6 - November 26, 1992.

Inuit Art from the Collection. Macdonald Stewart Art Centre, Guelph, Ontario. January 4 - August 1, 1993.

30   Janet Kigusiuq

Hands of a Giant, c. 1973

graphite and coloured pencil on paper

56 x 76 cm ⚓

Purchased with funds donated by Blount
Canada Ltd., with assistance from the
Ontario Government through the Ministry of
Citizenship and Culture, 1982

MS980.146

References:

Driscoll, Bernadette. *Inuit Myths, Legends and
Songs*. Winnipeg: Winnipeg Art Gallery, 1982,
p.39.

Exhibitions:

Inuit Myths, Legends and Songs. Winnipeg Art
Gallery. March 12 - May 2, 1982 (and tour),
cat. no. 24.

Contemporary Inuit Drawings. Macdonald Stewart
Art Centre, Guelph, Ontario. December 5, 1987
- February 7, 1988 (toured in Canada and the
United States in 1988-89), cat. no. 68.

*Contemporary Inuit Drawings from the Macdonald
Stewart Art Centre Collection*.
The Gallery/Stratford, Stratford, Ontario.
September 6 - November 26, 1992.

Stories that Janet Kigusiuq remembers from her childhood provide a wealth of inspiration for drawing. During the time that Jack and Sheila Butler were art advisors to the Sanavik Co-op, they invited Kigusiuq and others to use syllabic texts to explain the stories illustrated in their drawings. Of this startling image, dominated by two oversized hands, Kigusiuq said:

It is said that this giant used to kill people. Here are some people who are afraid because they are going to die. I hear that they were really very afraid. Here are the big hands of the giant. And he is about to kill. I do not know what else to say about it. I have finished writing. *

* Quoted in Bernadette Driscoll, *Inuit Myths, Legends and Songs* (Winnipeg: The Winnipeg Art Gallery, 1982), p.39.

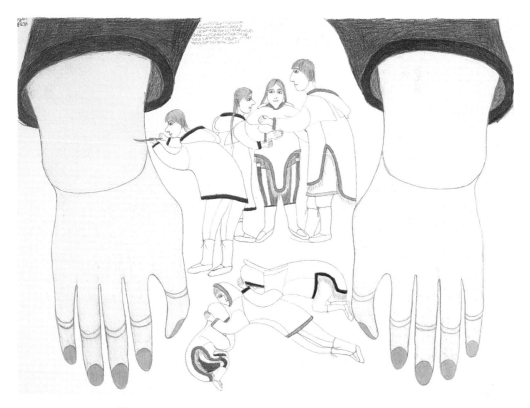

Janet Kigusiuq typically fills the entire drawing page with carefully controlled colour; the scale and boldness of her images attest to her unwavering confidence working in this medium. This haunting image of a boy and his dog, each with a piercing frontal gaze, is actually based on a playful theme, as Janet Kigusiuq explains:

These two are having a great time. They are running around, and the dog is running after the boy. I liked to play with dogs when I was younger. I really enjoyed that.*

* Janet Kigusiuq, Baker Lake Art Symposium, August 1994.

31   **Janet Kigusiuq**
Boy with Dog, 1992
graphite and coloured pencil on paper
56 x 76 cm ⊥
Purchased with funds donated by Blount Canada Ltd., 1993
MS993.030

Janet Kigusiuq's bold patterns of colour and energetic style are so engaging they tend to mask the significant cultural information contained in her drawings. Her interpretive comments about this drawing show her understanding of the behavioral patterns of the caribou, wolves, and birds that she portrays. This understanding was essential to survival in the traditional Inuit culture.

These are caribou eating. This hunter is planning to go shoot caribou with arrows. The wolf is following, and the other wolf is coming out of his den. And that bird up there is diving as birds sometimes dive. This is the tundra [coloured area filling right half and lower half of page], *and the space above is the sky.**

* Janet Kigusuiq, Baker Lake Art Symposium, August 1994.

32   Janet Kigusiuq
     Hunter with Caribou, 1992
     graphite and coloured pencil on paper
     56 x 76 cm ⏃
     Purchased with funds donated by Blount
     Canada Ltd., 1993
     MS993.031

Recalling her experience as a young girl of about twelve years, Janet Kigusiuq presents a portrait of the people of her camp in this drawing. They are resting or sleeping comfortably in their adjoining iglus in the Back River area around 1938.

Beginning with the alert figure seated in profile in the lower left and progressing clockwise, Janet Kigusiuq has identified the figures in this drawing as: (1) her mother, Jessie Oonark who was pregnant at the time with Peggy Qablunaaq; (2) her youngest sister, Mary Yuusipik, b. 1936; (3) her father, Qabloonak; (4) her sister, Miriam Nanurluk, b. 1932; (5) her sister, Victoria Mamnguqsualuk, b. 1930; (6) herself, b. 1926; (7 and 8) Mamak, who had just had a baby, and her husband, Innuqatsik; (9) Josiah Quinanguaq, b. 1928; (10) her brother Nuilaalik, b. 1928, who was adopted by her grandmother; and (11) her grandmother, Natak. Natak has the traditional facial tattoos though none of the younger women have chosen to have them.

33   Janet Kigusiuq
Oonark's Family Portraits in an Old Iglu in the Back River Area in 1938, 1993
graphite and coloured pencil on paper
56 x 76 cm
Purchased with funds donated by Blount Canada Ltd., 1993
MS993.032

34   Janet Kigusiuq

a)   *Back River Landscape #1*, 1993
     coloured pencil on paper
     56 x 76 cm
     Gift of Marie Bouchard, 1994
     MS994.017

b)   *Back River Landscape #2*, 1993
     coloured pencil on paper
     56 x 76 cm ⊥
     Purchased with funds donated by Blount
     Canada Ltd., 1993
     MS993.033

Janet Kigusiuq grew to adulthood north of Baker Lake in the Garry Lake and Back River area. As she explained to Marie Bouchard, Baker Lake art dealer, her recollections of the landscape of that area are still fresh in her mind.

I made these drawings from my memory. When I was a child, my family would move camp with each different season. These two drawings depict where my grandmother, Natak, and my brother Nuilaalik, who was adopted by her, would camp on the Back River in the summer. We would join them there to fish. We would get there by walking and by dog team.

Back River #1 is the view of the camp to the west. The small pool area to the left were the best spots for fishing. At the top are cliffs and hills.

Back River #2 is a view to the east. The gold and red coloured areas represent sandy areas where we would set up our tents. There are rocks on the hill top. *

* Janet Kigusiuq, explanation to Marie Bouchard, February 1995.

34b

34a

Armand Tagoona

Born 1926 at Repulse Bay, died 1991. Resided in Baker Lake and also lived in Chesterfield Inlet, Iglulik, Rankin Inlet and Arviat.

Considering his drawings as complete expressions in their own right, Armand Tagoona did not generally accompany his images with verbal interpretations. Noting this, George Swinton once commented:

Tagoona's drawings are fusions of thought and images, of memory and dreams, of past and present. The past is brought forward. It is made real through imagery. The logic of the image is its power to convince, its faculty to speak without the use of words. Words have other uses. Tagoona's drawings are drawn metaphors. *

* George Swinton in introduction to Armand Tagoona, *Shadows* (Ottawa: Oberon Press. 1975).

Armand Tagoona is the brother of Marjorie Esa. In 1959 he was ordained in Rankin Inlet as a deacon in the Anglican Church of Canada. The following year he was ordained to the priesthood and is acknowledged to be as the first Inuk to be ordained and Anglican priest. Ten years later he resigned from the Anglican Church and founded the Arctic Christian Fellowship. Armand Tagoona is also recognized as an author, having published *Shadows* in 1975. His drawings have been exhibited in solo exhibitions at the Robertson Galleries in Ottawa. Tagoona's work is in public collections including the Winnipeg Art Gallery, The Canada Council Art Bank, Ottawa, the Carleton University Art Gallery, Ottawa; the Museum of Civilization, Hull and the Joseph and Margaret Muscarelle Museum of Art, The College of William and Mary in Virginia, Williamsburg.

35 Armand Tagoona

Arctic Tears, c.1987

coloured pencil on paper

38 x 44.6 cm

Purchased with funds donated by Blount Canada Ltd., 1994

MS994.003

Exhibitions:

Baker Lake Drawing Retrospective. Isaacs/Inuit Gallery, Toronto, Ontario. April 23 - May 20, 1994.

Harold Qarliksaq

(Karleesuk; Qarlisaq; Quareliksaq; Qarliksaw; Quarliksaq; Kaleesuk; Kagliksak)

Born 1928 in the Back River/Garry Lake area, died 1980. Moved to Baker Lake in the early 1960s.

Harold Qarliksaq is best known for his drawings which he began in 1970 in order to supplement his trapping income. At the same time, he also produced sculpture and contributed to the print collections. His work has been featured in *Harold Qarliksaq Drawings*, Waddington Galleries, New York, 1979; *Harold Qarliksaq, Baker Lake Drawings*, Theo Waddington Inc., Montreal, 1980 and many group exhibitions including *Eskimo Games: Graphics and Sculpture/Giuochi Eschimesi: grafiche e sculture*, National Gallery of Modern Art, Rome, 1981 and *The Gift Collection of Frederick and Lucy S. Herman*, Joseph and Margaret Muscarelle Museum of Art, Williamsburg, Virginia, 1993. Among the public collections which hold his work are the National Gallery of Canada, Ottawa; The Canada Council Art Bank, Ottawa and the University of Alberta, Edmonton.

The delicate double line that characterizes Harold Qarliksaq's drawings is so distinctive it has become a type of signature for this unusual artist. Qarliksaq worked almost exclusively with graphite pencil, seldom incorporating colour into his soft, clearly-defined images.

This drawing depicts Inuit travelling on the land, moving to a new campsite, with the dogs as well as humans carrying packs. A lively vitality is conveyed in the active postures of the figures and in the open mouths of the dogs as they strain forward under their burdens.

36   Harold Qarliksaq

Migration, 1978

graphite on paper

56.5 x 76 cm

Purchased with funds donated by Blount
Canada Ltd., with assistance from
the Ontario Government through the Ministry
of Citizenship and Culture, 1980

MS980.139

Exhibitions:

L'Art Inuit de la Collection Macdonald Stewart Art Centre. Château Dufresne, Musée des Arts Décoratifs, Montreal, Quebec. December 9, 1982 - January 23, 1983.

A hunter all of his life, Harold Qarliksaq drew frequently on that experience for subject matter in his drawings. Here a successful hunter and his dog haul a slain caribou by *kamotik* (traditional wood-slat sled) from the hunting ground to the camp where his family waits.

Qarliksaq's precision in handling essential detail is evident in the care with which he depicted the lashings and knotting system securing the caribou carcass to the sled. The forward movement of the over-sized hunter, his arms swinging to enhance his momentum, imparts a dynamic energy to this carefully drawn image.

37 Harold Qarliksaq
Untitled (caribou hunting)
graphite on paper
38 x 56 cm ⊼
Purchased with funds donated by Blount
Canada Ltd., 1993
MS993.035

When travelling by dog team in the winter months, it was common practice for Inuit to stop periodically for a "mug up" of steaming tea to warm themselves and rest their dogs. In this drawing, Harold Qarliksaq presents four hunters gathered around a primus stove and tea kettle with their mugs while the dogs rest, still harnessed to the heavily-laden sleds.

The extraordinary focus on detail, considered important by Qarliksaq, is evident in the attention paid to the over-sized primus stove and the extreme care with which the artist made clear the harnessing system for the dogs. Each dog is harnessed to the sled by a separate, detachable trace. It is interesting to compare this drawing with Anguhadluq's drawing of dogsled travelling (No. 1).

38   Harold Qarliksaq
     Untitled (stopping for tea)
     graphite on paper
     56 x 76 cm ⊥
     Purchased with funds donated by Blount
     Canada Ltd., 1993
     MS993.036

In this tense hunting scene, Qarliksaq uses syllabic inscriptions to identify the *nuna* (land) at the top of the page and the *imoq* (water) at the bottom. On the land the hunter at the top left runs along the shore line in rapid pursuit of the caribou, his bow and arrow ready for use. At the same time, a kayaker on the lake throws a harpoon after the fleeing caribou, and even the dog and the fish seem involved in the chase. Under the fish at the lower centre of the page is the Inuktitut inscription, "The fish wants to bite the caribou."

Additional syllabic inscriptions at the top of the page give further insight into the dynamics of this drawing. The boy in the upper right corner, who seems to be hurried along by the adult hunter, exclaims, "He never even waits for me!"

The adult hunter pulling the young boy expresses his own distress in the syllabic inscription which seems to emanate from his mouth:

There it goes, the big bull caribou, down wind from us. It will smell us. Now we will never catch it. And there are no more caribou anywhere. We are very unfortunate. We've got no more arrows and no bullets. We are poor. We've got nothing."

39 Harold Qarliksaq
    Untitled (hunting caribou)
    graphite on paper
    56 x 76 cm
    Purchased with funds donated by Blount
    Canada Ltd., 1993
    MS993.037

Myra Kukiiyaut (Kookeeyout; Kookiemut; Kukeeyout; Kukiyaut; Kuukiyaut; Cookiemut)

Born 1929 in Baker Lake.

When Myra Kukiiyaut was a child, her family moved to a camp across Baker Lake. In 1956 they returned to live in the settlement of Baker Lake. In addition to producing drawings, prints, wall hangings and sculpture, Myra Kukiiyaut is an accomplished throat singer. Among her performances was an appearance at Expo '86. Kukiiyaut is also active in community affairs, having served as a Board member of the Sanavik Co-operative. Her first prints appeared in the 1971 *Baker Lake Print Collection*, and they have been included nearly every year since. More than 50 exhibitions have included Kukiiyaut's work. Examples are *Inuit Myths, Legends and Songs*, Winnipeg Art Gallery, 1983; and *Selections from the McMaster Art Museum Collection*, McMaster Museum of Art, Hamilton, Ontario, 1992. Her works are found at the Art Gallery of Ontario, Toronto; the Carleton University Art Gallery, Ottawa and The Joseph and Margaret Muscarelle Museum of Art, The College of William and Mary in Virginia, Williamsburg.

Myra Kukiiyaut's early life experience was shaped, to a large degree, by the presence in the Central Arctic of Christian missionaries and their teachings, although the spiritual aspects of traditional Inuit culture also provide inspiration for some of her graphic works. Of this drawing, she said:

I had no idea (no image in my mind) of a kavavauq or the monster-like ghost that Inuit used to scare their children. I have no idea what a kavavauq is like. I just drew those winged things to make the drawing look scary as much as possible. This person is supposed to be very smart, the person with the pana (snow knife) in front of his parka. Even before new religions were known to the Inuit, some people were able to overcome spirits or shaman's powers. Some men were very smart, and they would be able to overcome – through spiritual and mental effort – shamanism and spirits and things like that.

This man is overcoming spirits. The pana is very useful to him spiritually, but especially physically. He would use it against the cold weather for survival, to build a snow house. Physically, he would use it to defend himself from actual animals. Also, he is killing this spirit-bird image in the centre of the drawing. This knife can be used many different ways. It can be used to kill actual, natural animals or birds. The snow knife [on the bird in the lower right corner] is just to show that the snow knife can be used for different defenses. The man can use it to defend himself from any other living creature – physical or spiritual.*

* Myra Kukiiyaut, in interview with Marion Jackson and William Noah, Spring 1983.

40   Myra Kukiiyaut
     Untitled (hunter and spirit birds), 1974
     coloured pencil on paper
     50.3 x 66.2 cm
     Purchased with funds donated by Blount
     Canada Ltd., with assistance from
     the Ontario Government through the Ministry
     of Citizenship and Culture, 1980
     MS980.057

Exhibitions:

Inuit Drawings from the Macdonald Stewart Art Centre in Guelph. Oakville Galleries/Gairloch, Oakville, Ontario. November 19, 1986 - January 4, 1987.

Contemporary Inuit Drawings from the Macdonald Stewart Art Centre Collection. The Gallery/Stratford, Stratford, Ontario. September 6 - November 26, 1992.

Proud of the traditional skills of survival and conscious of the interdependence of gender roles in Inuit culture, Myra Kukiiyaut reflected on this drawing as follows:

This is a man, and this is a woman. They're just like any married couple – a man and a woman and a baby and so on. But the man was able to think in order to survive and feed his family. There are creature/things around, but this man is thinking. These animal images are not present but are in his mind – sort of a vision that he is able to concoct, knowing there are animals somewhere. That's why he has two heads, to show that he is an ordinary man but also that he is thinking these visions.

The fish can be understood two different ways. A man can kill a fish or kill an animal in order to support his family and vice versa. After the man kills and gives the fish or the meat to the woman, the woman can work on the meat or cook it and then give it to the man. So they are both giving to each other.

In the old days, the Inuit were very smart, especially the man supporting his family only on animals without the modern survival equipment. The women were really strong too in those days. They were able to look after their small kids and their grown kids too, as well as looking after themselves. At the same time, they would look after the bedding and would supply their families with firewood such as willow bush. And they would look after all the meat and the household, the general household. The men were not baby-sitters like nowadays. Everything now has changed, and everything is completely different from those days.

I think of the old days looking at these drawings. It's just like you were there now. *

* Myra Kukiiyaut, in interview with Marion Jackson and William Noah, Spring 1983.

41   Myra Kukiiyaut
Untitled (family and visions of animals), 1974
graphite and coloured pencil on paper
50.7 x 65.7 cm ⊥
Purchased with funds donated by Blount
Canada Ltd., with assistance from
the Ontario Government through the Ministry
of Citizenship and Culture, 1980
MS980.058
References:
"Qamanittuaq: Where the River Widens - Exhibition,
Symposium and Adventure. *Inuit Art Quarterly*
(Winter 1994): illustrated p.52.

Like many Inuit artists of her generation, Myra Kukiiyaut presents a narrative through the depiction of sequential episodes with an individual appearing more than once on a single page. As Kukiiyaut explains, the hunter is presented twice in this drawing:

This animal is going to go bite that lady, and this other person is going to go and attack to keep the animal from biting the lady. That is the same man; he was here [at the bottom of the page], *and then he went up there to help the lady. I just draw things out of my head; I don't draw stories that really happened.*

I used to draw pictures of songs that were sung by the old people, but now I just draw pictures that come out of my mind. I used to draw from songs. I still remember many of the songs. *

* Myra Kukiiyaut, in interview with Marion Jackson and Judith Nasby, October 1993.

42 Myra Kukiiyaut
Untitled (man saving woman from fierce animal), 1974
coloured pencil on paper
50.8 x 65.7 cm
Purchased with funds donated by Blount Canada Ltd., with assistance from the Ontario Government through the Ministry of Citizenship and Culture, 1980
MS980.060

When viewing her drawing in the autumn of 1993, Kukiiyaut commented that she did not really remember making this particular one. Nevertheless, she was able to comment on the subject matter and to reflect on the general inspiration for her graphic works. Her comments, as translated by her son, Matthew, follow:

This is about people turning into animals. I have never seen this happen myself. I just thought about it and made the drawing. I don't really know about people turning into animals. It is nothing that I heard.

I used to draw just from looking at the clouds in the springtime or the water – watching water's movements and the clouds. That's how I used to draw. We used to have a good window in our old house, and I would always look out the window at the water. Now we can't see the water, but that's what I used to do – look at the water.*

* Myra Kukiiyaut, in interview with Marion Jackson and Judith Nasby, October 1993.

43   Myra Kukiiyaut
Untitled (people turning into animals)
coloured pencil on paper
40.5 x 65.5 cm ⊥
Purchased with funds donated by Blount
Canada Ltd., 1993
MS993.041

Victoria Mamnguqsualuk

(Mummokshoarluk; Mammookshoarluk; Mumngshoaluk; Mumngusualuk)

Born November 1930 in the Back River/Garry Lake area. Moved to Baker Lake in 1963.

Victoria Mamnguqsualuk is a daughter of Jessie Oonark and a sister of Janet Kugusiuq, Nancy Pukingrnak and William Noah. She began making wall hangings in the earliest days of the Co-operative and started drawing about 1970. Many of her drawings have been used for prints and although she has done carving, drawing is her preferred medium. Her solo exhibitions were *The Long Night - Mamnguqsualuq of Baker Lake*, The Isaacs/Innuit Gallery, Toronto, 1983; *Victoria Mamnaguqsualuk Baker Lake Artist*, Northern Images, Whitehorse, 1984 and *Keeveeok Awake: Mamnuguqsauluk and the Rebirth of Legend at Baker Lake*, Ring House Gallery, Edmonton, 1986. Her wall hangings were featured in *Northern Lights: Inuit Textile Art from the Canadian Arctic*, The Baltimore Museum of Art, 1993-94. Examples of her work are in numerous public collections including the Anchorage Museum of History and Art; the Canadian Museum of Civilization, Hull; the Carleton University Art Gallery, Ottawa and the Inuit Cultural Institute, Rankin Inlet.

Mamnguqsualuk has written a text on the reverse side in Inuktitut syllabics:

It is said that a brother and a sister were the only people on the face of the earth. The third being was a dog. The young woman refused to marry her brother, so her father commanded her to marry their dog, saying, "This person refuses to take a husband, so this person must marry her dog." The daughter and her dog had many children. When the children grew up they ate too much, so the old man took them to an island. Every once in a while, the old man took some food to them. Because the mother of the dog children loved them, she told them, "When the old man comes to bring you food, lick his kayak (to show that you are hungry) and pounce on the old one."

Versions of this same story have been recorded in various parts of the Canadian Arctic, often with the conclusion that some of the children were set to sea on a raft made from the sole of a *kamik* (boot). This raft drifted to the south where the dog/human children settled and became the ancestors of the white race. See also Mark Uqayuittuq's presentation of this same theme (No. 28).

44 **Victoria Mamnguqsualuk**

A Legend, The Origins of the White Race, 1973

graphite and coloured pencil on paper

56.5 x 76 cm ⚓

Purchased with funds donated by Blount Canada Ltd., 1981

MS981.014

Exhibitions:

L'Art Inuit de la Collection Macdonald Stewart Art Centre. Château Dufresne, Musée des Arts Décoratifs, Montreal, Quebec. December 9, 1982 - January 23, 1983.

Contemporary Inuit Drawings from the Macdonald Stewart Art Centre Collection. The Gallery/Stratford, Stratford, Ontario. September 6 - November 26, 1992.

Inuit Art from the Collection. Macdonald Stewart Art Centre, Guelph, Ontario. January 4 - August 1, 1993.

Victoria Mamnguqsualuk's storytelling interest is again apparent in this drawing of a sequence of episodes from the story of the two young women who lived on each others lice. The story begins in the top left corner, progresses across the top of the page, and resumes in the lower left corner, continuing along the bottom of the page. Figures of the two young women and their male visitor are repeated in successive pictorial segments of the story. In a syllabic inscription on the verso, Mamnguqsualuk has explained this story:

Two girls were left behind in an old iglu. When they got hungry, they ate each others lice. On this they lived a for long time. Then, one day, they had a visitor. The visitor was curious to know what the girls had been eating. He killed them and opened their stomachs, and he found lice.

In other versions of this tale, the digested lice fly out, transformed into mosquitoes, to plague the visitor.

45 **Victoria Mamnguqsualuk**
Legend of The Women Who Lived on Each Other's Lice, 1973
mixed media on paper
56.5 x 75.5 cm
Purchased with funds donated by Blount Canada Ltd., 1981
MS981.017

Exhibitions:

Originale Inuit Tegninges fra Macdonald Stewart Art Centre, Canada. Musikhuset, Aarhus, Denmark. April 25 - May 15, 1984 (toured in Denmark).

Contemporary Inuit Drawings from the Macdonald Stewart Art Centre Collection.
The Gallery/Stratford, Stratford, Ontario. September 6 - November 26, 1992.

A story of epic proportion, the Qiviuq legend is known in various versions across the North American Arctic. A heroic figure similar to Homer's Ulysses, Qiviuq is known for travelling the world and embracing his many adventures with prodigious courage and uncanny imagination. In this drawing, Victoria Mamnguqsualuk presents an episode in which the mother of one of Qiviuq's many wives kills her daughter in an attempt to seduce Qiviuq. In a syllabic inscription on the verso, Mamnguqsualuk explains this drawing as follows:

An old woman had a daughter who was married to Qiviuq. While Qiviuq was hunting, the old woman, pretending to look in her daughter's hair for lice, murdered the girl. The old woman skinned her daughter's face and put the skin over her own face and tried to fool Qiviuq into thinking she was his wife. Qiviuq returned from the hunt and spent the night with the old woman wearing her daughter's face. Qiviuq was not fooled. On the following day, while the old woman was gathering willow branches, Qiviuq silently left her behind.

46   Victoria Mamnguqsualuk

Qiviuq's Mother-in-Law Kills her Daughter and Pretends to be the Daughter When Qiviuq Returns, 1973

graphite and coloured pencil on paper

56.1 x 75.8 cm ⚓

Purchased with funds donated by Blount Canada Ltd., with assistance from The Canada Council, 1980

MS980.151

Exhibitions:

Contemporary Inuit Drawings from the Macdonald Stewart Art Centre Collection.
The Gallery/Stratford, Stratford, Ontario.
September 6 - November 26, 1992.

Victoria Mamnguqsualuk provided a narrative text on
the reverse of this drawing in Inuktitut syllabics:

*It is said that two people were walking on the land. One fell through a hole in the earth, the
other was peeking through at his companion. Someone from below saw the person peeking
through the hole and bid the two to come down and join them. They went down. Whenever
the visitors would fall asleep, those from below would take bites out of them. The people
underground never slept. Because they never slept, the whites of their eyes were red.**

* Quoted in Bernadette Driscoll, *Inuit Myths, Legends and Songs*
(Winnipeg: Winnipeg Art Gallery, 1982), p.50.

47   **Victoria Mamnguqsualuk**
Legend of (Visiting) *Peoples in the Underworld,*
1973
graphite and coloured pencil on paper
55.7 x 75.7 cm
Purchased with funds donated by Blount
Canada Ltd., with assistance from The
Canada Council, 1980
MS980.152

During his travels, Qiviuq encountered the evil Naqaqongituk (the people with fleshless calves). During his narrow escape from these dangerous people, Qiviuq killed one of them. This drawing depicts the ensuing activities when the friends of the fallen Naqaqongituk pulled him back to camp and cannibalized his body. Mamnguqsualuk narrates the story in Inuktitut syllabics on the reverse of the drawing:

It is said that the people with fleshless calves were cannibals. They cut up the man that had become Qiviuq's victim for their food. They divided his parts for food. The victim was pulled away by his own friends and cut apart.

A little child entered into the presence of a woman and said, "I am eating my father's kidney." This woman exclaimed to the child, "Oh, was it your father that they cut apart?" As he licked his father's back, the child said, "Yes, it was my father that has been cut apart."

Mamnguqsualuk's mother, Jessie Oonark, also made drawings about Qiviuq's encounters with the Naqaqongituk (No. 6).

48   Victoria Mamnguqsualuk
Eaten by Cannibals, 1973
graphite and coloured pencil on paper
56 x 76.4 cm
Purchased with funds donated by Blount
Canada Ltd., with assistance from The
Canada Council, 1980
MS980.153

Mamnguqsualuk was in her 30s by the time she moved into Baker Lake, and her memories of life on the land remain a rich inspiration for her graphic works. Noting these memories as a source for this particular drawing, Mamnguqsualuk explained:

The figures at the top are men hunting and chasing caribou with their kayaks. The one in the corner – after his kayak tipped over – is ready to climb back on top again. The two ladies in the centre on the right are pulling a willow bush. The one in the bottom [right] corner is drilling something with Inuit tools. The man on the other side is after a wolf. These are from my experience.*

* Victoria Mamnguqsualuk, in interview with Marion Jackson and William Noah, Spring 1983.

49 Victoria Mamngusualuk
    Untitled (hunting caribou and working), 1975
    graphite and coloured pencil on paper
    55.8 x 76.3 cm
    Purchased with funds donated by Blount
    Canada Ltd., with assistance from The
    Canada Council, 1980
    MS980.042
Exhibitions:
*Inuit Drawings from the Macdonald Stewart Art
    Centre in Guelph*. Oakville Galleries/Gairloch,
    Oakville, Ontario. November 19, 1986 - January
    4, 1987.
*Contemporary Inuit Drawings from the Macdonald
    Stewart Art Centre Collection.*
    The Gallery/Stratford, Stratford, Ontario.
    September 6 - November 26, 1992.

Hannah Kigusiuq (Keegoaseat; Keegooseeot; Keegooseot; Keyousikuk; Kuuk)

Born 1931 in the Garry Lake area. Moved to Baker Lake in 1957.

Hannah Kigusiuq started to draw during the 1960s. Although she makes wall hangings, most of her work has been done in the print or drawing media. She has been a frequent contributor to the Baker Lake print collections and her work has been included in numerous group exhibitions such as *Baker Lake Prints and Print-Drawings: 1970-1976*, Winnipeg Art Gallery, 1983, *The World Around Me*, University of Lethbridge Art Gallery, 1988 and *Inuit Drawings*, Inuit Gallery of Vancouver, 1990. Kigusiuq's work is in the permanent collections of a number of art museums including the Amon Carter Museum of Western Art, Fort Worth; the University of New Brunswick, Fredericton; the Carleton University Art Gallery, Ottawa; the Winnipeg Art Gallery and the Joseph and Margaret Muscarelle Museum of Art, the College of William and Mary in Virginia, Williamsburg.

In this scene of an active winter camp, Hannah Kigusiuq depicts the myriad of activities that engaged Inuit families living on the land in the winter time. Aiding the viewer in understanding these activities, she has provided syllabic transcriptions to identify figures, give voice to their thoughts and identify their actions. Beginning with the woman at the entrance to the iglu at the centre top of this drawing and progressing clockwise, the syllabic transcriptions are translated as follows:

Woman at entrance to iglu: *A woman cleaning up the iglu*

Figure crouching beside iglu: *"I need to go (to urinate)!"*

Woman with load on back: *A woman carrying willow bush for the cooking fire*

Small child in lower right corner: *"Father!"*

Figure in shelter: *A young person went to get water for cooking*

Object near dog in lower centre: *Caribou's hoof*

Small seated child in centre of drawing: *"Mother!"*

Man running, near bottom left corner: *"Look, there's a big wolf!"*

Woman running behind him: *"Where?"*

50 Hannah Kigusiuq

Untitled (domestic scene with iglu), 1975

graphite on paper

53 x 75.2 cm

Purchased with funds donated by Blount Canada Ltd., 1980

MS980.054

References:

Nasby, Judith. *The Role of Drawing in Inuit Art*. University and College Art Gallery Association of Canada, Calgary, Alberta, 1994. (publication forthcoming) fig. 19.

Exhibitions:

Contemporary Inuit Drawings from the Macdonald Stewart Art Centre Collection. The Gallery/Stratford, Stratford, Ontario. September 6 - November 26, 1992.

Hannah Kigusiuq identifies the general subject of this drawing to be
that of invoking spiritual aid in a time of need:

*In the old days, some people used to be angakok or shamans. The (kneeling figure) in the
middle there is a shaman. The helpers are the half-seal/half-human images. When the
shamans and their families were very hungry or starving, the shamans would perform, and
they would get help from the animals. The polar bear is there because the shaman
performed, and that performance got this bear. I don't really know whether the helpers
themselves turn into animals. I just drew them from my mind, half-animals, from the way
that I heard the stories and the way I thought the drawing should be. And I was half-scared
at the time, so I just drew those images there to make the drawing look interesting.
Sometimes when I read – especially from the section of Revelations in the Bible – the story
and the way it is told seems similar to the shaman helpers.**

* Hannah Kigusiuq, in interview with Marion Jackson and William Noah, Spring 1983.

51   Hannah Kigusiuq
Shaman and Helpers
graphite on paper
56.4 x 76.2 cm ⏳
Purchased with funds donated by Blount
Canada Ltd., with assistance from
the Ontario Government through the Ministry of
Citizenship and Culture, 1980
MS980.145

Exhibitions:

*L'Art Inuit de la Collection Macdonald Stewart Art
Centre.* Château Dufresne, Musée des Arts
Décoratifs, Montreal, Quebec. December 9, 1982
- January 23, 1983.

*Inuit Drawings from the Macdonald Stewart Art
Centre in Guelph.* Oakville Galleries/Gairloch,
Oakville, Ontario. November 19, 1986 -
January 4, 1987.

By filling her drawing pages with a large number of lively figures engaged in activities of traditional Inuit culture, Hannah Kigusiuq provides a window into the life she remembers from her days on the land. In this drawing, two figures [the framed faces in the upper right] literally look through windows, the windows of a snow house, to view the varied activities of winter camp life. As Kigusiuq explains:

This is how they used to live years ago. These two people [framed faces] are looking through a hole in the iglu. These women [the three just to the left of centre] are playing together, and their children [bottom centre] are sledding. And these two children [left of the children sledding] are pretending to fight.*

* Hannah Kigusiuq, Baker Lake Art Symposium, August 1994.

52 **Hannah Kigusiuq**
    Untitled (camp)
    graphite on paper
    57 x 77 cm ⊼
    Purchased with funds donated by Blount
    Canada Ltd., with assistance from
    the Ontario Government through the Ministry
    of Citizenship and Culture, 1987
    MS987.002

The memory of travelling on the land by dog team remains very strong in Hannah Kigusiuq's mind. In this lively drawing, she depicts Inuit and their dogs together pulling a heavy *kamotik* (sled) as was sometimes done in "the old days." Explaining the various activities represented in this drawing she has said:

I drew those images from my memory – from my mind – the way we used to travel. There is a special word – qomoraqtuq – for three dogs with people pulling in the front. I myself have not done this pulling in the front, only from the side of the sled. While they are travelling – the whole family travelling together on the sleds – when they would stop for a rest and a meal, the young people would go up to the hills and slide down for a while. By the time I was born, they were already using modern rifles. When the family travelling on the sled stopped for a rest, the man would go up to the hill to look out for some caribou.

The syllabic inscriptions read as follows:

Upper left: *The little child is going up a hill, and the grandmother is watching. She has a baby in front of her amoutiq.*

Left centre: *"Stop! Sit down! Stop! Halt!" (command to dogs)*

Lower centre: *"My little daughter fell off the sled!"*

Lower right: *The little one who fell off the sled*

*Hannah Kigusiuq in interview with Marion Jackson and William Noah, Spring 1983.

53   Hannah Kigusiuq
     Qomoraqtuq (dog teams), 1978
     graphite on paper
     56.2 x 76 cm
     Purchased with funds donated by Blount
     Canada Ltd., with assistance from the
     Ontario Government through the Ministry of
     Citizenship and Culture, 1980
     MS980.144

References:
Jackson, Marion. "Inuit Drawings: More than Meets
     the Eye," *American Review of Canadian Studies*
     27:1 (1987):37.

Exhibitions:
Inuit Drawings and Sculptures. Cedar Ridge Studio
     Gallery, Scarborough, Ontario. March 6 - 9,
     1984.

Ruth Qaulluaryuk

(Kaoluaayuk; Kaoloaryuk; Kowlagee; Qalluaryuk; Qauluaryuk; Qualluaryuk; Qaulluarjuk; Qualluryuk)
Born 1932 in the Back River/Garry Lake area. Moved to Baker Lake in the 1960s.

Ruth Qaulluaryuk is the daughter of Luke Anguhadluq. She is known for her drawings, prints and particularly her wall hangings, which were featured in the major exhibition *Northern Lights: Inuit Textile Art From the Canadian Arctic* organized by The Baltimore Museum of Art, 1993-94. Since she began to draw in 1970, her work has been represented in more than 30 exhibitions including *The Inuit Stamp/L'estampe inuit*, Department of Indian Affairs and Northern Development and the National Museum of Man, 1977-82; *Baker Lake Prints & Print-Drawings: 1970-1976*, Winnipeg Art Gallery, 1983 and *Uumajut: Animal Imagery in Inuit Art*, Winnipeg Art Gallery, 1985. The list of permanent collections which hold her work includes the Canadian Museum of Civilization, Hull; the National Gallery of Canada, Ottawa and the Prince of Wales Northern Heritage Centre, Yellowknife.

Ruth Qaulluaryuk frequently depicts the tangled patterns of ground willow that grows so abundantly in the Baker Lake area. This interest in patterns of vegetation is so pronounced that Qaulluaryuk often treats the tundra as the subject, rather than the background of her images. She has said:

I don't really know what to say about this drawing, but I have drawn the tundra because I like the tundra. I like looking at musk ox so I drew the muskox. I also like the snowy owl. I would like to become a muskox because, when I look at the tundra, it looks so delicious when they (the willows) are growing. These two images are eggs.*

* Ruth Qaulluaryuk, Baker Lake Art Symposium, August 1994.

54 Ruth Qaulluaryuk

Ookpik, 1993

graphite and coloured pencil on paper

72.2 x 57.2 cm ⊥

Purchased with funds donated by Blount Canada Ltd., 1993

MS994.002

Exhibitions:

Women Who Draw. Feheley Fine Arts, Toronto, Ontario. November 13 - December 31, 1993.

Simon Tookoome (Tacoomie; Tukummik; Hiutinuaq)

Born 1934 in the Gjoa Haven area. Moved to Baker Lake in 1969.

Using the medium of drawing to convey information about traditional Inuit culture, Simon Tookoome has explained his drawing of shamanic transformation as follows:

This is a shaman forming himself into a wolf. A shaman can sort of transform himself – or form himself into an image of a wolf. Those two things sticking out through his mouth are showing that his tongue can stretch out into a fork. And his hands are bitten by wolf spirits. Even if you can't see – or have never seen – shaman's spirits, you can see them in this drawing. Even if you cannot see them, you can understand them in his drawing.*

* Simon Tookoome, in interview with Marion Jackson and William Noah, Spring 1983.

On arriving in Baker Lake, Simon Tookoome became a member of the printshop where he worked as a printer and stonecutter. Tookoome is known for sculpture and drawings as well as prints. He has worked for the Inuit Broadcasting Corporation as a cameraman and interviewer. At Expo '86 he competed in the traditional games, demonstrating his widely recognized skills with the traditional Inuit dogsled whip. He has also contributed to more than 100 exhibitions including *Contemporary Inuit Art at the National Gallery of Canada*, 1965; *Eskimo Narrative*, Winnipeg Art Gallery, 1979 and *Simon Tookoome: Original Drawings*, the Albers Gallery, San Francisco, 1993. Among the numerous galleries holding his work are the Inuit Cultural Institute, Rankin Inlet; the Carleton University Art Gallery, Ottawa; the Canadian Guild of Crafts, Montreal and the Winnipeg Art Gallery.

55 Simon Tookoome

Untitled (wolf spirits), 1974

graphite and coloured pencil on paper

50.5 x 66 cm

Purchased with funds donated by Blount Canada Ltd., with assistance from the Ontario Government through the Ministry of Citizenship and Culture, 1980

MS980.066

References:

"Qamanittuaq: Where the River Widens - Exhibition, Symposium and Adventure. *Inuit Art Quarterly* (Winter 1994): illustrated p.52.

Exhibitions:

Contemporary Inuit Drawings. Macdonald Stewart Art Centre, Guelph, Ontario. December 5, 1987 - February 7, 1988 (toured in Canada and the United States in 1988-89). cat no. 70.

Contemporary Inuit Drawings from the Macdonald Stewart Art Centre Collection. The Gallery/Stratford, Stratford, Ontario. September 6 - November 26, 1992.

Steeped in the traditions of Inuit culture, Simon Tookoome frequently weaves complex ideas together within a seemingly simple image. In this drawing, he portrays the process of thinking and also represents Inuit concepts of the creation of humans and animals. Tookoome explained the drawing as follows:

The Inuit, especially a long time ago, used to think and to visualize – to have a vision of going out hunting, hunting wolves especially. This man is thinking, thinking to go out and hunt wolves or maybe to get wolves to be his pets. The person on top could be a shaman or from a story.

This drawing has two stories. When people used to tell stories about the creation of nature or the earth – that [image on the top of the man's head] *shows how it was. The animals and humans lived very closely. Nothing was wild. The reason the person has an animal body and a human head is because a shaman would have a helper, a spirit helper.*

You can see many images on both sides [radiating from the central figure], *and they are part of his thoughts. They are not real things. They are just thoughts. This person is all by himself and he is deep in thought. It is the same thing for me. I can see things in my thoughts. For anyone who has a proper consciousness, your thoughts are where your mind brings your memories and your plans together.* *

* Simon Tookoome, in interview with Marion Jackson, William Noah, and Judith Nasby, October 1993.

56   Simon Tookoome
Isumavuq (A Person in Thought), 1975
coloured pencil on paper
50.6 x 66 cm
Purchased with funds donated by Blount
Canada Ltd., with assistance from
the Ontario Government through the Ministry
of Citizenship and Culture, 1980
MS980.106

Simon Tookoome's drawings are complex and incorporate not just superficial description but also the wisdom embodied in traditional Inuit culture. His discussion of this drawing gives insight into the complex interplay between the traditional camp leader and the other members of the camp:

These are people living out on the land. We used to train wild wolves out on the land, sort of like pets.

That's a group of people. One of the two heads is the leader, and the rest are the people who live in that camp. They are talking together, preparing, deciding whether to go fishing or hunting. The decision is made by the leader, and they are having a meeting before. The general procedure was that the leader would talk with the people before doing anything or deciding anything. The Inuit never had written pages or laws, but the procedure was that they had a leader to guide them.

The group at the campsite used to follow the leader. This is a general expression of leadership, not just one specific leader. The leader goes and the whole family follows. *

* Simon Tookoome, in interview with Marion Jackson, William Noah, and Judith Nasby, October 1993.

57   Simon Tookoome
The Hunters Planning, 1987
coloured pencil on paper
56 x 76 cm ⊥
Purchased with funds donated by Blount Canada Ltd., with assistance from the Government of Ontario throught the Ministry of Citizenship and Culture, 1987
MS987.007
References:
Nasby, Judith. "A Report on the Baker Lake Art Symposium." *Eskimo N.S.*, no. 49 (Spring/Summer 1995) illustrated.

In this compelling image, Simon Tookoome has been able to merge an expression of the creation myth, shamanism, and dream thoughts. This drawing has complex and overlapping meanings as explained by Tookoome:

This drawing has three meanings to it. The first one, a long time ago, the people and the animals used to be close together. They understood each other. Secondly, a shaman used to have a helper. That spirit was inside the person. Thirdly, it is just a story. Sometimes a person goes to sleep and dreams about unusual things. So this has three meanings.

Of all of my artwork, the story of this drawing is the strongest one I have. The reason why it is so powerful and so strong is because it can be translated into Inuit stories like traditional stories, but it can be translated into Biblical stories, like creation. Adam and Eve lived closely with the animals and could touch them. In the Inuit legends, it is the same story. Secondly, the shaman used to be very respected by all the people.*

Tookoome is pleased that this powerful image is one that has been silk-screened onto sweatshirts produced at the Jessie Oonark Arts and Crafts Centre.

I like the image on the sweatshirt and am glad my work will be spread out more, and my artwork will be known by many people.*

* Simon Tookoome, in interview with Marion Jackson, William Noah, and Judith Nasby, October 1993.

58   Simon Tookoome
The Story, 1993
coloured pencil on paper
56 x 76 cm ⊼
Purchased with funds donated by Blount
Canada Ltd., 1993
MS993.027

Ruth Annaqtuusi Tulurialik (Annaqtusii; Annuktoshe; Annaqtussi; Anattose)
Born 1934 in Kazan River area. Since her adoption as an infant by her uncle, she has resided in Baker Lake.

Ruth Annaqtuusi Tulurialik has lived in the vicinity of Baker Lake all her life. She was adopted by her uncle, Thomas Tapatai, who was the Inuit assistant to the Anglican missionary. As a child, Tulurialik enjoyed hearing the stories and experiences of Inuit who came in from the land to trade and visit the mission. She also enjoys camping herself and is extremely interested in recording the old ways through her drawings. Of this drawing she has said:

These people are out fishing. The one – the biggest image – is catching fish and trying to survive on fishing alone. The one [upper left corner] is drum dancing, and the woman is singing. The woman is singing one of the Inuit songs, an Inuktitut song. You can see the sounds. That is a seal [in the lower left corner]. Only a few times in the years – like maybe every two years or so – will seals come up to Baker Lake – but then only a few. There are hardly any seals in Baker Lake. It's fresh water.*

* Ruth Annaqtuusi Tulurialik, in interview with Marion Jackson and William Noah, Spring 1983.

About 1971, Ruth Annaqtuusi Tulurialik began her career as an artist making drawings. Her other media include printmaking and wall hangings. She co-authored the book *Qikaaluktut: Images of Inuit Life* with David F. Pelly in 1986. Both Annaqtuusi and her husband, Hugh Tulurialik, are musicians who often perform in the community. Her work has been represented in many exhibitions including *The Vital Vision: Ruth Annaqtuusi Tulurialik*, Art Gallery of Windsor, 1986-87; *Drawing and Selected Prints: Ruth Annaqutuusi Tulurialik, Baker Lake*, The Upstairs Gallery, Winnipeg, 1987 and *The People Within – Art from Baker Lake*, Art Gallery of Ontario, 1976. Among the galleries holding her work are the Canadian Guild of Crafts, Montreal; the McMaster Museum of Art, Hamilton; the Carleton University Art Gallery, Ottawa and the Art Gallery of Windsor.

59　Ruth Annaqtuusi Tulurialik
Untitled (cleaning a fish), 1975
graphite and coloured pencil on paper
56.2 x 75.6 cm ⊥
Purchased with funds donated by Blount
Canada Ltd., 1980
MS980.047

Some of the happiest times in the old days were when Inuit from isolated camps would come together for celebration. This busy drawing captures many of the activities and also the lively energy of such mid-winter gatherings. Ruth Annaqtuusi Tulurialik explained:

This is the Inuit way of having a celebration. Everybody is gathering at a camp for a celebration. The figure with the heads coming out from between the fingers is a shaman performing shamanism. The little images are spirits coming out through her hands. It is a woman shaman.

*In the lower right corner, a woman is helping to cover some snow over the iglu on the outside to make it warmer. In the top left corner, the figures are doing rope gymnastic games. This man on the right is a man skinning a caribou.**

* Ruth Annaqtuusi Tulurialik, in interview with Marion Jackson and William Noah, Spring 1983.

60   Ruth Annaqtuusi Tulurialik

Two Iglus, 1975

graphite and coloured pencil on paper

56 x 76.2 cm ⊼

Purchased with funds donated by Blount Canada Ltd., with assistance from the Ontario Government through the Ministry of Citizenship and Culture, 1980

MS980.048

References:

Jackson, Marion E. and David Pelly. *The Vital Vision: Drawings by Ruth Annaqtuusi Tulurialuk*. Windsor: Art Gallery of Windsor, 1986, pp. 15 and 17.

Exhibitions:

The Vital Vision: Drawings by Ruth Annaqtuusi Tulurialuk. Art Gallery of Windsor, Windsor, Ontario. February 23 - March 30, 1986, no. 18.

Inuit Drawings from the Macdonald Stewart Art Centre in Guelph. Oakville Galleries/Gairloch, Oakville, Ontario. November 19, 1986 - January 4, 1987.

While times of gathering were generally very happy (No. 3, 14), this particular gathering is troubled by the uneasy discord of haunting spirits. Tulurialik explained the drawing thus:

The people are gathering somewhere – in a haunted place. They're sort of scared or afraid of something, afraid of the spirits. This is one of the spirits in the top left corner. I know of places like this, like those tornaqtiliq (haunted islands) down southeast of Baker Lake. I've never been there. I would be afraid to go there. But I have heard stories about that place. Some people have lost some of their equipment there. Some people have gotten really sick. And some of the hunters have lost some of their dogs there, especially the leader dogs.*

* Ruth Annaqtuusi Tulurialik, in interview with Marion Jackson and William Noah, Spring 1983.

61 Ruth Annaqtuusi Tulurialik
    Scene (gathering in a haunted place), 1977
    graphite and coloured pencil on paper
    56 x 76.2 cm
    Purchased with funds donated by Blount
    Canada Ltd., with assistance from
    the Ontario Government through the Ministry of
    Citizenship and Culture, 1980
    MS980.138

References:

Jackson, Marion E. and David Pelly. *The Vital Vision:
    Drawings by Ruth Annaqtuusi Tulurialuk.*
    Windsor: Art Gallery of Windsor, 1986, pp.15
    and 17.

Exhibitions:

*The Vital Vision: Drawings by Ruth Annaqtuusi
    Tulurialuk.* Art Gallery of Windsor, Windsor,
    Ontario. February 23 - March 30, 1986, no. 19.

62   Ruth Annaqtuusi Tulurialik
      Untitled (hunting on the land in summertime),
      1977
      graphite and coloured pencil on paper
      56 x 76.1 cm ⌁
      Purchased with funds donated by Blount
      Canada Ltd., with assistance from The
      Canada Council, 1982
      MS982.175

References:

Jackson, Marion E. and Judith Nasby. *Contemporary
      Inuit Drawings*. Guelph, Ontario: Macdonald
      Stewart Art Centre, 1987, p.16.

Nasby, Judith. *Contemporary Inuit Drawings/Dessins
      inuit contemporains*. Guelph, Ontario:
      Macdonald Stewart Art Centre, 1989 (exhibition
      catalogue, abridged version) no. 5, p.9.

Exhibitions:

*L'Art Inuit de la Collection Macdonald Stewart Art
      Centre*. Château Dufresne, Musée des Arts
      Décoratifs, Montreal, Quebec. December 9,
      1982 - January 23, 1983.

Contemporary Inuit Drawings. Macdonald Stewart
      Art Centre, Guelph, Ontario. December 5, 1987
      - February 7, 1988 (toured in Canada and the
      United States in 1988-89), cat. no. 72.

*Contemporary Inuit Drawings from the Macdonald
      Stewart Art Centre Collection*.
      The Gallery/Stratford, Stratford, Ontario.
      September 6 - November 26, 1992.

Because Ruth Annaqtuusi Tulurialik has lived in Baker Lake all of her life and worked for a time as a translator at the nursing station, she has heard many stories of the starvation on the land. She was acutely aware of the sick and starving people who were brought into Baker Lake during the 1950s and envisions the experience of starvation in this drawing which she explains as follows:

These people are out hunting in the land, and they lack food and are half-starving. That's why one of the men is in the lake or in the river trying to go across to go on the land and kill the caribou. These figures surrounding the caribou are ganging up on one caribou so they can kill it. The man with the bow and arrow is carrying one of his children on his shoulders, and there is a woman following. *

* Ruth Annaqtuusi Tulurialik in interview with Marion Jackson and William Noah, Spring 1983.

Marjorie Esa (Isa; Iisa; Essa)

Born 1934 at Nuqsarnaarjuk (near Iglulik). Since being adopted as an infant, she has lived most of her life in Baker Lake.

During the Art Symposium in Baker Lake in Summer 1994, Marjorie Esa used this drawing to discuss her own motivations and methods for drawing.

As I was looking out the window one day, I was trying to think of how I could help my husband, and that's how I started drawing. When I would go out on the land for a walk, I would stop off and wait for the birds to come so I could see the colours of the birds. I like birds, and that's why I draw birds.

We also hunt birds for food. Whenever I myself would catch a bird such as a ptarmigan or any other bird, I would lay it on the floor and sketch the bird. Whenever I caught a fish, I would lay it on the floor also and sketch the fish. They are not always the same!

I have tried to draw people, but I have been told that my people look very sick – so I just decided to draw birds. I like birds so much. *

* Marjorie Esa, Baker Lake Art Symposium, August 1994.

Marjorie Esa is the sister of Armand Tagoona who is also represented in this exhibition. Esa began drawing around 1971 and had a solo exhibition *Isa Drawings* in 1974 at the Canadian Guild of Crafts in Montreal. Her prints, wall hangings, sculpture and drawings have been featured in approximately 35 other exhibitions including *Uumajut: Animal Imagery in Art*, Winnipeg Art Gallery, 1985; *Inuit Drawings*, Inuit Gallery of Vancouver, 1990 and *Drawings and Sculpture from Baker Lake*, Winnipeg Art Gallery, 1992-93. Among the many public collections which include Esa's work are the Joseph and Margaret Muscarelle Museum of Art, The College of William and Mary in Virginia, Williamsburg; the Winnipeg Art Gallery and the Art Gallery of Ontario, Toronto.

63 Marjorie Esa
Birds, 1972
coloured pencil on paper
52.5 x 75 cm ⊥
Purchased with funds donated by Blount
Canada Ltd., 1993
MS993.028

References:

Nasby, Judith. *The Role of Drawing in Inuit Art*. University and College Art Gallery Association of Canada, Calgary, Alberta, 1994. (publication forthcoming).

Irene Avaalaaqiaq (Tiktaalaaq; Ahvalakiak; Ahvalaquaq; Avalakiak; Avaalaqiaq)

Born 1941, Wharton Lake (Kazan River area). Moved to Baker Lake in 1958.

Irene Avaalaaqiaq began drawing around 1970. Although her major medium is wall hangings, she also makes sculpture and has had prints in the Baker Lake collection. She has shown in numerous Canadian and international exhibitions, such as *Wall Hangings: Embroidered and Appliquéd by Ahvalakiak of Baker Lake*, Isaacs/Inuit Gallery, Toronto 1973; *Master Artists of the 1970's*, The Inuit Gallery of Vancouver Ltd., 1980; *Baker Lake Prints & Print-Drawings 1970-76*, Winnipeg Art Gallery, 1983 and *Northern Lights: Inuit Textile Art from the Canadian Arctic*, The Baltimore Museum of Art, 1993-94. She is represented in such major public collections as the Montreal Museum of Fine Arts; the Prince of Wales Northern Heritage Centre, Yellowknife; the Carleton University Art Gallery, Ottawa; the Agnes Etherington Art Centre, Kingston and the National Gallery of Canada, Ottawa.

Relating this image to a story, Irene Avaalaaqiaq explained that this drawing represents a sequence of actions.

There's a story that a person was standing on a shoreline or somewhere waiting for a giant fish to come along and swallow him. The giant fish came along and swallowed the person, and, as the person was being swallowed, the person turned into a bird or maybe a fish. This is one image (i.e., a single giant fish) in movement. Out here [lower right corner of the drawing], the fish is starting to swallow a person. There [just above the first image], it goes inside; and out here [left side of drawing], the bird is coming out of the giant fish. As it comes out, you can see it. The lines on the fish show the movement of the fish through the water. I got the idea of a human face (for the giant fish) because somebody on the shoreline was pretending to be a human. One thing I was going to make was an island, but the paper is so small that it cannot include every little detail of the story.*

Marion Tuu'luuq also drew inspiration from this story of the fish that swallows people (No. 19) as did Mark Uqayuittuq (No. 27).

* Irene Avaalaaqiaq, in interview with Marion Jackson and William Noah, Spring 1983.

64   Irene Avaalaaqiaq
Story of the Fish that Swallows People, 1971
coloured pencil on paper
56 x 76 cm
Purchased with funds donated by Blount Canada Ltd., with assistance
from the Ontario Government through the Ministry of Citizenship and Culture, 1980
MS980.149
Exhibitions:
L'Art Inuit de la Collection Macdonald Stewart Art Centre. Château Dufresne, Musée des Arts Décoratifs, Montreal, Quebec. December 9, 1982 - January 23, 1983.
Contemporary Inuit Drawings. Macdonald Stewart Art Centre, Guelph, Ontario. December 5, 1987 - February 7, 1988 (toured in Canada and the United States in 1988-89), cat. no. 27.
Contemporary Inuit Drawings from the Macdonald Stewart Art Centre Collection. The Gallery/Stratford, Stratford, Ontario. September 6 - November 26, 1992.

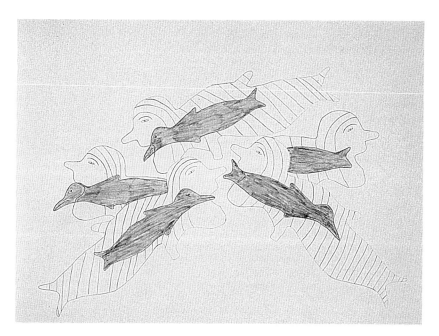

In autumn 1993, Irene Avaalaaqiaq identified this drawing as one she had
made "quite a long time ago" and said of this image:

I was thinking of willow bushes or greens. When you look at the ones with the
lines going up like "V", they are the live ones, growing ones. The leaves facing
down are the ones that are dying.

This [blue area at the bottom] is the water, and these are plants on the top.
The white areas at the bottom show where the snow is; the plants are dying because it's
cold and because of the snow. In the summertime, the plants grow up. In the fall,
the plants or anything growing starts to die.

I didn't bother to colour the leaves and the willow. *

* Irene Avaalaaqiaq, in interview with Marion Jackson, William Noah, and Judith Nasby, October 1993.

65 Irene Avaalaaqiaq
Willow Bushes
graphite and coloured pencil on paper
38.5 x 55.5 cm
Purchased with funds donated by Blount
Canada Ltd., 1993
MS993.047

In providing interpretation for this image, Irene Avaalaaqiaq alluded to the visual problems she effectively solved in this drawing. She has given expression to the thoughts in a person's mind and has portrayed the movement of the person's head glancing from side to side. Avaalaaqiaq's explanation follows:

You can see there is a great big head image here. The smaller images you see inside the big image are things – like thoughts – inside the person's head or brain. The images you see in the centre are that person's thoughts. When you are out on the land alone, sometimes something like a rock or something seems to move and makes you think you see a bird or a human or something. It is kind of scary sometimes – imagination! The thing is not really there, but you think you see it. As soon as it gets dark out there when I am out hunting or out camping, I get really scared or frightened.

My drawings are mostly from the experience of my lifetime, and some are from stories from my grandmother. These are thoughts during the night, and the green area around the head is an interpretation of the land. The person is looking in both directions, back and forth. *

Both Françoise Oklaga (No. 24) and Simon Tookoome (No. 56) concern themselves with representing thoughts, and their drawings provide valuable comparisons with Avaalaaqiaq's drawing.

* Irene Avaalaaqiaq, in interview with Marion Jackson, William Noah, and Judith Nasby, October 1993.

66   Irene Avaalaaqiaq

Imagination Visions

coloured pencil on paper

56 x 42 cm ⚓

Purchased with funds donated by Blount Canada Ltd., 1993

MS993.048

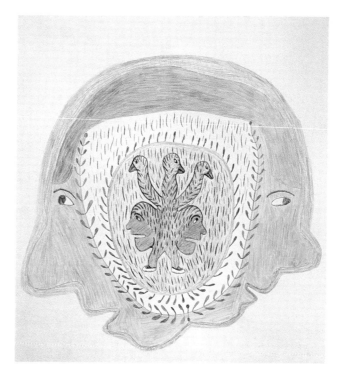

As Irene Avaalaaqiaq's comments suggest, recollections of her own experiences of seeing snowy owls on the land led her to a free association of ideas. Avaalaaqiaq explains that this complex drawing combines remembered experience, the sense of fear she has experienced on the land, and dreams of transformation.

When you are walking out on the land someplace, it is easy to see all sorts of plants and willow bushes. These images are the snowy owls that you see out on the land. It is a story. These are the snowy owls between the human faces, and the only choice they had was to turn into humans, become human.

Another way to think about it is that the person is scared and wanted to turn into a snowy owl. The colours that you see in the faces – turning blue and then into red – is to show that the person is really scared and wants to turn into a snowy owl. The person is really scared!

My grandmother used to tell me stories about wild life or wild birds, especially snowy owls, that sounded just like a human in the nighttime when they would make sounds. They would sound just like a human who was crying out, the sound of a person.

If it were possible, I wouldn't mind turning into a bird when I get scared, and I would just fly away! I really envy the little birds, the little wild birds, who move around and look down on you from the sky!*

* Irene Avaalaaqiaq, in interview with Marion Jackson, William Noah, and Judith Nasby, October 1993.

67   Irene Avaalaaqiaq
Snowy Owl Turning into a Person/Person Turning into Snowy Owl
coloured pencil on paper
56 x 76 cm
Purchased with funds donated by Blount Canada Ltd., 1993
MS993.049

Nancy Pukingrnak (Aupaluktuq; Aupalutuk; Pookertnak; Pookootna; Pukingnaaq; Pukingnerk; Pukingnark; Pukingnak; Pukinnak)

Born 1940 in the Back River area. Moved to Baker Lake in 1958.

Nancy Pukingrnak was encouraged by her mother, Jessie Oonark, to make carvings, wall hangings and crafts in the early 1960s. By 1971 Pukingrnak was making drawings and has since made several prints. Her participation at the Sanavik Cooperative has included being a member of the Board. A solo exhibition, *Nancy Pukingrnak: Baker Lake Drawings and Sculptures*, was held in 1976 at The Upstairs Gallery in Winnipeg. Her work has also been part of numerous group exhibitions including *Inuit Myths, Legends and Songs*, Winnipeg Art Gallery, 1982-83 and *Grasp Tight the Old Ways: Selections from the Klamer Family Collection of Inuit Art*, Art Gallery of Ontario, 1983-85. Her work can be viewed at the McMaster Museum of Art, Hamilton; the Canadian Museum of Civilization, Hull; the Carleton University Art Gallery, Ottawa and the Art Gallery of Nova Scotia, Halifax.

Nancy Pukingrnak enjoys drawing to convey traditional legends. She has said:

This is a story. These men with kayaks [upper left corner] are hunters. And this woman [upper right corner] is preparing seal clothing to make her granddaughter look like a seal. Down here [lower right corner] the granddaughter is being trained to dive under the water for a long period of time so that she can get those hunters who are being mean to her grandmother and herself. Later on she will pretend to be a seal and guide those hunters down to the ocean. And when the wind picks up – the strong wind – these men will drown. *

Pukingrnak's syllabic inscriptions aid in the interpretation of the story:

[Top left] *These are hunters preparing to seal hunt. A young woman is pretending to be a seal.* [Top right] *These men were planning to kill this young woman. A woman made clothing to make her look like a seal, and she pretends to be a seal.* [Bottom] *As she went far down to the deep sea, she's ready to kill them all.*

* Nancy Pukingrnak, in interview with Marion Jackson and William Noah, Spring 1983.

68 Nancy Pukingrnak
   Story of the Young Woman Disguised as a Seal,
   1974
   graphite and coloured pencil on paper
   56.4 x 75.9 cm
   Purchased with funds donated by Blount
   Canada Ltd., with assistance from
   the Ontario Government through the Ministry
   of Citizenship and Culture, 1980
   MS980.046
Exhibitions:
*Contemporary Inuit Drawings from the Macdonald
Stewart Art Centre Collection.*
The Gallery/Stratford, Stratford, Ontario.
September 6 - November 26, 1992.

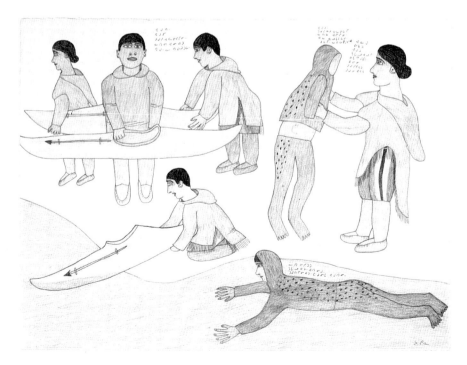

In the inland area around Back River where Nancy Pukingrnak spent her childhood, fish were often the only source of food. In the lower right corner of this drawing, Pukingrnak shows the men, wearing only their skin pants in the cold river water, building a stone weir to trap fish. Also pictured are men setting a line for drying the fish and a woman cleaning the fish. Summer tents on the left border of the drawing establish this as a summer campsite. Pukingrnak confirmed that this drawing records the old ways.

This is how we lived. We worked with our hands to get our food. That is what this picture is all about – working with our hands to get food. And we used to dry our food also as it's drawn there.*

* Nancy Pukingrnak, Baker Lake Art Symposium, August 1994.

69   Nancy Pukingrnak
     Untitled (drying fish), 1975
     graphite and coloured pencil on paper
     50.9 x 66 cm
     Purchased with funds donated by Blount
     Canada Ltd., 1980
     MS980.063

In addition to drawing from traditional legends and her own life experiences, Nancy Pukingrnak frequently allows her imagination to determine the content of her images. She has made soapstone sculptures and coloured pencil drawings, and consciously looks to her own past works for themes and ideas to develop further. Pukingrnak said of this drawing:

This is out of my imagination. One time I was making a soapstone carving. I was making a figure of a person, and the stone had lumps on the back of it, and that's how it turned out (i.e., with faces on the back). By thinking of that carving, I made these images. When I was chopping the soapstone, those figures automatically appeared in the stone. The shapes seemed to be easy to make into faces. I made those extra faces - just to make the figures look scary.

At first when I started out making drawings, I started out with sleds, images of sleds and dogs or whatever from experience. Then I though that I would do the legends. It was very much later on that I started making imagination drawings.*

* Nancy Punkingrnak, in interview with Marion Jackson and William Noah, Spring 1983.

70   Nancy Pukingrnak
     Untitled (spirit figures and hunters stretching skins), 1973
     graphite and coloured pencil on paper
     56.4 x 76.1 cm
     Purchased with funds donated by Blount Canada Ltd., with assistance from The Canada Council, 1982
     MS982.176
References:
Nasby, Judith. *The Role of Drawing in Inuit Art.* University and College Art Gallery Association of Canada, Calgary, Alberta, 1994. (publication forthcoming) fig. 8.

Pukingrnak sometimes creates images in which she tries to express the fear she has experienced in the face of the unknown and the imagined when camping out on the land.

This I drew out of my own mind. I am scared a lot, and this is a scary scene. These people [upper right] are eating themselves, and they are vomiting also. And this lady can hear all these (multi-headed creatures outside) as her husband sleeps. Because they are getting ready for bed, this child is peeing. That's all – I just drew it!*

Ruth Annaqtuusi Tulurialik and Irene Avaalaaqiaq have undertaken similar exploration of the unease one can feel when ones imagination takes over on the land (No. 61, 67).

* Nancy Pukingrnak, Baker Lake Art Symposium, August 1994.

71   **Nancy Pukingrnak**
     Untitled (iglu scene with green monsters),
     early 1970s
     graphite and coloured pencil on paper
     56.2 x 76.1 cm ⊥
     Purchased with funds donated by Blount
     Canada Ltd., with assistance from
     The Canada Council, 1983
     MS983.004

References:

Jackson, Marion E. and Judith Nasby. *Contemporary Inuit Drawings*. Guelph, Ontario: Macdonald Stewart Art Centre, 1987, p.26.

Exhibitions:

Originale Inuit Tegninges fra Macdonald Stewart Art Centre, Canada. Musikhuset, Aarhus, Denmark. April 25 - May 15, 1984 (toured in Denmark).

Contemporary Inuit Drawings. Macdonald Stewart Art Centre, Guelph, Ontario. December 5, 1987 - February 7, 1988 (toured in Canada and the United States in 1988-89), cat. no. 77.

In this beautifully drawn image, Nancy Pukingrnak expresses traditional Inuit cultural values as well an understanding for the tensions between generations ubiquitous in human nature. She has said of this work:

This is a scene where the man and woman are just talking, doing nothing. And the grandmother is telling them that they shouldn't be just doing nothing. The man should be out hunting, and the woman should be sewing. *

Note that Pukingrnak has drawn wavy lines from the mouth of the grandmother to the ears of the two young people, indicating that her words go to the ears but are ignored. The old woman's admonition, as inscribed in Inuktitut syllabics read as follows:

Stop wasting your time. Start sewing, cooking, cleaning up inside the iglu. If you do these things, you will have a long life ahead. If you just pay attention to each other, you will not have a future. Set a good example for other people. It is good to like someone, but there is a time for work.

* Nancy Pukingrnak, Baker Lake Art Symposium, August 1994.

72   Nancy Pukingrnak
     Untitled (grandmother's advice), 1985
     graphite and coloured pencil on paper
     56 x 76 cm ⊥
     Purchased with funds donated by Blount
     Canada Ltd., 1993
     MS993.042

The meeting of cultures is apparent in this drawing in which an Inuk in traditional skin clothing stands in front of an iglu and extends his ungloved hand in greeting to a *qabloonaq* (non-Inuit) who is wearing European dress and stands in front of a wood-frame house. The dialogue between the two captures a tension in this meeting:

Qabloonaq:

I am a White man, and I come from the world where trees are growing. I've heard that there are Inuit in a beautiful land where there is a clean environment. I will be giving a lot of money to you and building new houses in this land. I will have everything here in this beautiful land. I really envy the Inuit land and environment. I notice that you have big muscles when I shake hands with you in agreement so I can take your land. Where there are no trees, it is a good land. Inuit call it their own land. God gave me a land with trees that belongs to us white people. But in the trees, you can't look far away and see the distance.

Inuk:

We've heard and learned from the White people that there is Jesus and God, but it's the White people who do the bad things, things that do not agree with God's plan. God gave land for White people down in the South and land for the Inuit in the North. That is how I live as an Inuk – in the cold environment on the land. I live here. I use caribou skin for clothing. God gave us this land to live in where the weather is cold. But you White men live in the warmer land. When you came to my land, I shook hands with you. But later on, you called my land "your land." Your land has trees, and my land has no trees. I live in a cold land where I live in the iglu. God gave me this cold land. It's a beautiful land.

73   Nancy Pukingrnak
Untitled (Meeting between Inuk and
Qabloonaq), 1984
graphite and coloured pencil on paper
56 x 76 cm
Purchased with funds donated by Blount
Canada Ltd., 1993
MS993.043

William Noah

Born 1944 in the Back River area. Moved to Baker Lake in 1958.

William Noah is a son of Jessie Oonark and brother of Janet Kigusiuq, Victoria Mamnguqsualuk and Nancy Pukingrnak, all of whom are represented in this exhibition. Noah has been President of the Sanavik Co-operative, Chair of the Board of the Canadian Arctic Producers Ltd. in Ottawa, a Member of the Legislative Assembly of the Northwest Territories and a manager and a director of the Inuit Broadcasting Corp. He is currently employed at the Jessie Oonark Arts and Crafts Centre, Baker Lake. He began drawing in 1963 and although his work has appeared as prints, his primary medium is drawing. The first exhibition in which his work was shown was *Arctic Values '65*, New Brunswick Museum, Saint John. Among later exhibitions were *Eskimo Narrative*, Winnipeg Art Gallery, 1979; *Inuit Masterworks: Selections from the Collection of Indian and Northern Affairs Canada*, McMichael Canadian Collection, 1983 and *Qamanittuaq: The Art of Baker Lake*, National Gallery of Canada, 1991. His work is part of The McMichael Canadian Art Collection, Kleinburg; the Carleton University Art Gallery, Ottawa and the Montreal Museum of Fine Art.

William discusses this drawing:

This is Sugarloaf Mountain. When I look out the window from my office, I see it every day. I just drew this sometime in August. It is just a mountain, but it became famous a year- and-a-half ago. There was a woman who walked to Sugarloaf Mountain; she made the walk to help the poor people in Baker Lake. It had never really come to my mind before, but she went out there walking in February - February 14, Valentine's Day. That's the time she walked out there, but this drawing is summer scenery. It became a famous mountain, so I decided to draw it in a summer scene. Also, you can see a telephone pole and wires there.

This is the view out of my office window. You can see Baker Lake and a little island. It's gentle scenery. I made this with wax coloured pencils, several colours.

From here to the top of Sugarloaf Mountain it would be 25 or 26 miles. That woman was helping the people who are living in poverty, the people who are living on welfare and cannot make it to the next assistance check. It's really hard for the big families. If you have a big family, it is impossible to make it to the next assistance. She collected some money but mostly food and clothing - from the community and other communities and from across Canada as well as the United States. The woman was Susan Toolooktook.*

* William Noah, artist's statement, October 1993.

74 William Noah

Sugarloaf Mountain, 1993
coloured pencil and ink on paper
35.5 x 43 cm
Purchased with funds donated by Blount
Canada Ltd., 1993
MS993.022

This is from my own experience, repeated experience every summer. Food with tea or coffee tastes really good outside! After being in town or being inside for a long time during a harsh winter, when spring comes or the summer comes we go out there just to enjoy. Especially after the rain, everything smells good. The food tastes great. And the land is really fresh after the rain.

As you can see, there is a rainbow up there and the clouds. Right after the rain, the sun really comes out. You just go out there to enjoy being on the land. Here there is a square biscuit, a cup of tea, and bannock. This drawing gives an impression of people who bring fancy stuff nowadays, like a silver serving plate with handles! On the land there are blueberries and there are bones that have been chipped off and eaten by wolves or foxes. And that's an inukshuk [in the centre] – just giving the impression that it's nice to be out there.

This is not a particular place. It is an interpretation of scenery – just an impression of enjoying the land. After the rain, the air is fresh and the plants smell good and make you really hungry. The first thing that comes to your mind is tea, and biscuit, and bannock. With the blueberries, it is late August. That's the best time of the year!*

* William Noah, artist's statement, October 1993.

75   William Noah
Tea, Bannock and Biscuit, 1993
coloured pencil and ink on paper
42.5 x 35.5 cm ⊥
Purchased with funds donated by Blount
Canada Ltd., 1993
MS993.023

Those are the lake trout drying. What we do is let the skin or the outside dry first. As soon as that is completely dry, we turn it inside out and let the inside meat dry. Those are the fillets on the ground, and those are two tents [in the background].

76   William Noah

Drying Fish at Kikiktauja, 1993
coloured pencil and ink on paper
24 x 27 cm ⌁
Purchased with funds donated by Blount
Canada Ltd., 1993
MS993.024

Spring camp – we called it "fish camp." It used to be the RCMP spring fish camp, but nowadays everybody goes to that camp, to do some fishing, or camping or just to enjoy. It is straight across from the town. It is only about 15 miles from town. We normally travel by boat or skidoos, but we can't travel there with Hondas. We call it "Kikiktauja". It is on a small island where two rivers come down into a lake.

Some people just go out there now to catch fish and bring the fish into town, but this is how we used to do it. My relatives would usually dry the fish. If I weren't working, I would plan to go out there for at least two weeks.

This was an actual photograph, and I just drew it on the paper. Recently, the things I have been doing are photograph-images. Sometimes I change the landscape a little bit. I have bundles and bundles of photographs. I do a lot of landscapes, campsites, animals, and fish. I don't do very much of shamanism or the people themselves. I just like to do a lot of landscapes from memories. These are the things that I see every day.

Some things that I saw are really hard to put into words or images, but other things like fish are easy to draw. Fish, caribou, landscapes are easier to draw because I see them almost every day. But other things are harder to draw – like I can't really draw a house, a drawing of a house or iglu for some reason.

I would like to be out there now, just getting the feeling of the beach itself. That way, your mind relaxes more and makes it easier to create images. Of course, I put stronger colours, but you can recognize that this is generally of nature.

In the Inuit way of living, you have to associate with the land, mountains, hills and even the sky. Otherwise, you will get really frustrated and you won't really know what is wrong with you. That is the only way to be peaceful, to create a rest in your mind. The town cannot relax you. The people cannot give you peace, but when you are out there, you come back refreshed. People may think you would get lonely out there, but that is the wrong impression. I think the people who are lonely are the people who never go out of the community or who are in the big cities. I think they are the most unlucky people.*

* William Noah, artist's statement, October 1993.

DRYINGFISH BY William Noah 1993

This is the Prince River area – Prince River Mountain there [in the centre]. Of course, the land has changed since the photograph was taken and the drawing was made. The Prince River runs [from the left of the page] – that's the mouth of the river running down into Baker Lake. Today, instead of those tents, there are two cabins there and another cabin further down and one on the point there. That's a person [in the boat] checking fish nets, catching char or lake trout. That's me checking nets.

Visitors or tourists sometimes go to Prince River to do a little fishing. It's a good view of the land. Every spring we go there just to go camping or to cut some caribou meat to dry it out or to make some dry fish. It's everybody's favourite spot to go to in the springtime. It's about twelve to fourteen miles east of town, along the shore of Baker Lake. It's easy to get there, no matter what the condition of the weather. We go by Honda or by skidoo.

That's Prince River Mountain in the middle. It's really high – nice, beautiful land. The top is only about 30 or 40 yards wide; it's really small on the top. That's a person on the top signalling that there are caribou out there. There are two caribou walking by, walking toward Baker Lake. The small little things on the horizon are markers made of rocks – inukshuks. It's so far – a long distance.

It's a good place to go for tea or for a picnic. It's everybody's favourite spot. *

* William Noah, artist's statement, October 1993.

77   William Noah
Prince River - Spring Camp Area, 1992
coloured pencil and ink on paper
56 x 76 cm ⊥
Purchased with funds donated by Blount
Canada Ltd., 1993
MS993.025

SELECT BIBLIOGRAPHY

Baker Lake Annual Print Collection Catalogues. 1970, 1971, 1972, 1973, 1974, 1975, 1976, 1977, 1978, 1979, 1980, 1981, 1982, 1983/84, 1985, 1986, 1987, 1990.

Birket-Smith, Kaj. *The Caribou Eskimos: Material and Social Life and Their Cultural Position*. Report of the Fifth Thule Expedition 1921-24, vol. 5. Copenhagen: Gyldendal, 1929.

Blodgett, Jean. *Tuuluq - Anguhadluq*. Winnipeg: Winnipeg Art Gallery, 1976.

Blodgett, Jean. *The Coming and Going of the Shaman: Eskimo Shamanism and Art*. Winnipeg: Winnipeg Art Gallery, 1978.

Blodgett, Jean and Marie Bouchard. *Jessie Oonark: A Retrospective*. Winnipeg: Winnipeg Art Gallery, 1986.

Briggs, Jean. *Never in Anger*. Cambridge: Harvard University Press, 1970.

Bryers, Joanne Elizabeth. "The Graphic Art of the Baker Lake Eskimos from July 1969 to July 1973." Master's thesis, University of Toronto, 1974.

Butler, K.J. "My Uncle Went to the Moon." *artscanada* 30: 184-187, (1973-74): 154-58.

Butler, Sheila. "The First Printmaking Year at Baker Lake: Personal Recollections." *The Beaver* outfit 307:1 (Spring 1976): 17-26.

Butler, Sheila. Untitled essay in *Baker Lake Prints and Print-Drawings*, 1970-76. Winnipeg: Winnipeg Art Gallery, 1983: 13-17.

Butler, Sheila. *Baker Lake Prints and Print-Drawings* 1970-76. Winnipeg: Winnipeg Art Gallery, 1982.

Cook, Cynthia Waye. *From the Centre: The Drawings of Luke Anguhadluq*. Toronto: Art Gallery of Ontario, 1993.

Colakovic, Marina R. "Mytho-Poetic Structure in the Inuit Tale of Kivioq the Wanderer (Inuit Story-telling in the Light of Oral Literature Theory)." Occasional paper. Guelph: Macdonald Stewart Art Centre, 1993.

Driscoll, Bernadette. *The Inuit Amautik: I Like My Hood To Be Full*. Winnipeg: Winnipeg Art Gallery, 1980.

Driscoll, Bernadette. *Inuit Myths, Legends & Songs*. Winnipeg: Winnipeg Art Gallery, 1982.

Driscoll-Engelstad, Bernadette. "A Woman's Vision, A Woman's Voice: Inuit Textile Art from Arctic Canada," *Inuit Art Quarterly* 9:2 (1994): 4-13.

Elderfield, John, *The Modern Drawing: 100 Works on Paper from the Museum of Modern Art*. New York: Museum of Modern Art, 1983.

Fernstrom, Katharine W. and Anita E. Jones. *Northern Lights: Inuit Textile Art from the Canadian Arctic*. Baltimore: The Baltimore Museum of Art, 1993.

Fry, Jacqueline. *Baker Lake Prints and Drawings*. Winnipeg: Winnipeg Art Gallery, 1973.

Goetz, Helga. *The Inuit Print/L'estampe inuit*. Ottawa: National Museums of Canada, 1976.

Harper, Francis. *Caribou Eskimos of the Upper Kazan River, Keewatin*. Lawrence, Kansas: University of Kansas, 1964.

Houston, Alma. *Inuit Art: An Anthology*. Winnipeg: Watson and Dwyer, 1988.

Jackson, Marion Elizabeth. "Baker Lake Inuit Drawings: A Study in the Evolution of Artistic Self-Consciousness." Ph.D. diss., University of Michigan, 1985.

Jackson, Marion E. and Judith M. Nasby. *Contemporary Inuit Drawings*. Guelph: Macdonald Stewart Art Centre, 1987.

Jackson, Marion E. and William Noah. "Artists' Interpretations and Syllabic Translations for the Laker Lake Drawings in the Collection of the Macdonald Stewart Art Centre." manuscript. Guelph: Macdonald Stewart Art Centre, 1983.

Jackson, Marion and David Pelly. *The Vital Vision: Drawings by Ruth Anaaqtuusi Tulurialik*. Windsor: Art Gallery of Windsor, 1986.

Leroux, Odette. "Three Decades of Inuit Printing: Evolution and Artistic Trends 1958-1988" in *In the Shadow of the Sun: Perspectives on Contemporary Native Art*. Hull: Canadian Museum of Civilization, 1993: 495-533.

Mendelowitz, Daniel M. *Drawing*. New York: Holt, Rinehart and Winston, 1967.

Moore, Charles H. "Anguhadluq's Art: Memories of the Utkuhikhalingmiut." *Études/Inuit/Studies* 2:2 (1978): 3-21.

Moore, C.H. *Keeveeok, Awake! Mamnguqsualuk and the Rebirth of Legend at Baker Lake*. Edmonton: Ring House Gallery, University of Alberta, 1986.

Nasby, Judith. *Contemporary Inuit Drawings/Dessins Inuit contemporains*. Guelph: Macdonald Stewart Art Centre (exhibition catalogue, abridged version), 1989.

Nasby, Judith. *Contemporary Inuit Drawings: The Gift Collection of Frederick and Lucy S. Herman*. Williamsburg, Virginia: Muscarelle Museum of Art, College of William and Mary, 1993.

Nasby, Judith. "Revealing the Truth of the Artist's Hand: Contemporary Inuit Drawing." *Inuit Art Quarterly* 9:3 (Fall 1994): 4-13.

Nasby, Judith. "Collections: Macdonald Stewart Art Centre," *Inuit Art and Crafts* 2 (December 1984): 34-41.

Opperman, Hal N. "The Inuit Phenomenon in Art-historical Context," *Inuit Art Quarterly* 1:2 (1986): 1-4.

The People Within/Les gens de l'intérieur. Toronto: Art Gallery of Ontario, 1976.

Rasmussen, Knud. *Intellectual Culture of the Iglulik Eskimos*. Report of the Fifth Thule Expedition 1921-24, vol. 7, no. 1. Copenhagen: Gyldendal, 1929.

Rasmussen, Knud. *Intellectual Culture of the Caribou Eskimos*. Report of the Fifth Thule Expedition 1921-24, vol. 7, nos. 2 & 3. Copenhagen: Gyldendal, 1930.

Rasmussen, Knud. *The Netsilik Eskimos: Social Life and Spiritual Culture*. Report of the Fifth Thule Expedition 1921-24, vol. 9. Copenhagen: Gyldendal, 1932.

Routledge, Marie. *Inuit Art of the 1970s/L'art inuit actuel: 1970-79*. Kingston: Agnes Etherington Art Centre, Queen's University, 1979.

Swinton, George. *Inuit Sculpture*. Toronto: McClelland & Stewart, 1992.

Tagoona, Armand. *Shadows*. Ottawa: Oberon Press, 1975.

Tulurialik, Ruth Anaaqtuusi and David F. Pelly. *Qikaaluktut: Images of Inuit Life*. Toronto: Oxford University Press, 1986.

Vallee, F.G. *Kabloona and Eskimo in the Central Keewatin*. Ottawa: Northern Coordination and Research Centre, Department of Northern Affairs and National Resources, 1961.

Vastokas, Joan. "Continuities in Eskimo Graphic Style." *artscanada* 28: 162-163 (1971-72): 69-83.

Watson, Scott. Review of *Land, Spirit, Power: First Nations at the National Gallery of Canada* in *Canadian Art* 10:1 (1993): 34-43.

INDEX OF ARTISTS

PHOTO CAPTIONS

Page 4, Left: Summer camp in area of Chantrey Inlet (?), c.1930s. Note the sealskin tent and combination of fur clothing as well as evidence of manufactured trade goods such as the stove, cooking pots and items of clothing. *Photo courtesy of the Hudson's Bay Company Archives.*

Page 4, Right: Winter camp scene in Keewatin District, c.1930s. *Photo courtesy of the Hudson's Bay Company Archives.*

Page 8: Baker Lake, 1994 (photo by Verne Harrison)

Page 11, Left: Artists (from left to right) Marion Tuu'luuq, Marjorie Esa, Irene Avaalaaqiaq and Ruth Annaqtuusi Tulurialik in a group discussion held in the Community Centre where the exhibition *Qamanittuaq: Where the River Widens* was shown. Baker Lake Art Symposium, 1994. (photo by Stephen Robinson)

Page 11, Right: Baker Lake, view from the porch of the Jessie Oonark Arts and Crafts Centre, 1994. (photo by J. Nasby)

Page 12: Marion Tuu'luuq, artist; Judith Nasby, MSAC Director and David Tagoona, Mayor cutting a sinew rope to open the exhibition *Qamanittuaq: Where the River Widens* at the Baker Lake Art Symposium, 1994. (photo by Dave Sutherland)

Page 13: Artists (from left to right) Janet Kigusiuq, Myra Kukiiyaut, Hannah Kigusiuq, Ruth Qaulluaryuk, Nancy Pukingrnak and Victoria Mamnguqsualuk. Baker Lake Art Symposium, 1994. (photo by Dave Sutherland)

Page 14: Winnie Owingayak wears an elaborately beaded caribou *amautiq* showing the distinctive Baker Lake design during a history of clothing presentation. Baker Lake Art Symposium, 1994. (photo by J. Nasby)

Page 15, Left: Artist Myra Kukiiyaut displays a drawing in her home, 1993. (photo by J. Nasby)

Page 15, Right: Artist Simon Tookoome, Baker Lake Art Symposium, 1994. (photo by Nancy Campbell)

Page 16, Left: William Noah in his studio at the Jessie Oonark Arts and Crafts Centre, Baker Lake, 1993. (photo by J. Nasby)

Page 16, Right: Baker Lake, October 1993. (photo by J. Nasby)

Page 18: Armand Tagoona's house in Baker Lake, 1969. *Photo courtesy of the late Reverend Armand Tagoona.*

Page 19: Group portrait of the young men who built the first community hall in Baker Lake, c.1960 or 1961. This photograph may have been taken in front of the first school in Baker Lake. Back row left to right: William Noah, David Ananaut, Samson Aknauyuk, Peter Aningnik (Victoria Mamnguqsualuk's son), Peter Sevooga, Edwin Evo, Goadee Goadee, David Tagoona, Mr. McMaster (teacher); Middle row left to right: Bill Kashla, Barnabas Qudjak, James Tiringunguak, Hugh Avatituq, John Tapatai, Barnabas Situraq, Harold Etegoyok; Front row left to right: Hugh Ikoe, Charlie Toolooktook, Michael Alerk, David Toolooktook. *Photo courtesy Ilitsijaqturvik School, Baker Lake.*

Page 21: Three young men standing in front of the old Sanavik Co-op building in Baker Lake, early 1970s. Left to right: James Tiringunguak, Thomas Sivuraq, William Noah. *Photo courtesy of the late Reverend Armand Tagoona.*

Page 24: Baker Lake, 1983, showing the prefabricated frame homes in the community which had grown to a population of approximately 1,000 permanent residents by the early 1980s. (photo by Marion Jackson)

Page 27: Jessie Oonark with three of her daughters and Elizabeth Quinmnuq during a visit to Baker Lake, c.1955. Note that all are wearing Scottish tams available through the Hudson's Bay Company which were popular with Inuit women during the 1950s. Left to right: Mary Yuusipik, Jessie Oonark, Nancy Pukingrnak, Peggy Qabloonaq, Elizabeth Quinumnuq. *Photo courtesy of Ruth Annaqtuusi Tulurialik.*

Page 28: Baker Lake, c.1946, showing the Anglican Mission and the summer tents of visiting Inuit. *Photo by T. H. Manning, courtesy of the Hudson's Bay Company Archives.*

Page 29: Dog team travelling in Keewatin District, c.1930s. *Photo courtesy of the Hudson's Bay Company Archives.*

Page 32: Anglican Mission at Baker Lake, c.1950s. *Photo courtesy of Ruth Annaqtuusi Tulurialik.*

Page 33: Inuit catechist Thomas Tapatai, and Anglican missionary, the Reverend Smith, Baker Lake, c.1950s. *Photo courtesy of Ruth Annaqtuusi Tulurialik.*

Page 37: Artist Marion Tuu'luuq describing one of her drawings in the exhibition *Qamanittuaq: Where the River Widens* with interpreter Joan Killulark. Baker Lake Art Symposium, 1994. (photo by Dave Sutherland)

EXHIBITION ITINERARY

Baker Lake Community Centre
Baker Lake, Northwest Territories
August 18 - 24, 1994

Macdonald Stewart Art Centre
Guelph, Ontario
April 27 to September 10, 1995

Memorial University Art Gallery
St. John's, Newfoundland
January 12 to March 3, 1996

Winnipeg Art Gallery
Winnipeg, Manitoba
September 14 to November 17, 1996

McIntosh Gallery
University of Western Ontario
London, Ontario
January 9 to February 9, 1997

Carleton University Art Gallery
Ottawa, Ontario
February 18 to April 13, 1997

©Macdonald Stewart Art Centre, 1995
358 Gordon Street, Guelph, Ontario N1G 1Y1
Printed in Canada
All Rights Reserved

Canadian Cataloguing in Publication Data
Macdonald Stewart Art Centre
Qamanittuaq: Where the River Widens:
Drawings by Baker Lake Artists

Catalogue of an exhibition held at the Baker Lake
Community Centre, N.W.T., Aug. 18 - Aug. 24, 1994
and travelling to other galleries.
Includes bibliographical references and index.
ISBN 0-920810-57-8

1. Inuit - Northwest Territories - Baker Lake - Drawing - Exhibitions.
2. Macdonald Stewart Art Centre - Exhibitions.
I. Jackson, Marion E. (Marion Elizabeth).
II. Nasby, Judith, 1945 - .
III. Noah, William, 1944 - .
IV. Baker Lake Community Centre.
V. Title.

NC142.B34M3 1995741.9719'4C95-930929-2

Exhibition Curators:
Marion Jackson, Judith Nasby and William Noah
Catalogue Design:
Julie Gibb and Christian Morrison, GreenStreet Design
Printing:
C.J. Graphics Inc., Toronto
Photography of drawings:
Office for Educational Practice, University of Guelph, Julianna Murphy,
    Martin Schwalbe.
Copy Editing:
Stephen Robinson and Anne McPherson
    The catalogue text is set in Goudy Sans and the Inuktitut syllabics are
    created using Igalaat for Windows.
Cover:
Tundra near Kazan Falls, August, 1994 (photo by Verne Harrison).

The Macdonald Stewart Art Centre is supported by its sponsors - the
University of Guelph, the Wellington County Board of Education, the County
of Wellington and the City of Guelph, by memberships and donations and by
grants from the Ontario Government through the Ministry of Culture, Tourism
and Recreation and the Ontario Arts Council, and from the Federal
Government through The Canada Council and the Museums Assistance
Program of Canadian Heritage.